Harold R. Lowder

I wish to thank Ms. Mildred Mayne, Clinical Psychologist, for her professional guidance on the chapter, "Entertaining Your Children," as well as Ms. Barbara McEnroe for patiently typing and retyping the manuscript. Also those friends who encouraged me to write this book when I first faced the bleak prospect of being Suddenly Single.

This book is dedicated to all the women from whom I learned everything I know that enables me to live a full, comfortable life as a single man.

Library of Congress Catalog Card Number: 73-79914

International Standard Book Number: 0-8129-0369-2

Interior design by: Paddy Bareham, Planned Production

Contents

Introduction

Suddenly Single! That's the only way to describe it. You may be a husband whose marriage has been deteriorating for years and you've decided to call it quits. Perhaps you're a single young man finally leaving the protective custody of your parents' home. However long it took you to reach this point of moving out on your own, it takes only a minute, sitting in a strange bedroom, to realize that, from here on in, it's all going to be different. You're alone. All by yourself. *Single!*

Your suitcase isn't unpacked and nobody's going to unpack it for you. Where do you put what in which drawers? That's assuming you have drawers to put something in. Maybe you're getting hungry. What do you feel like eating? Yours is the only stomach you've got to worry about and right now you're the only person who's going to worry about it. How about breakfast tomorrow morning? Lunch on a rainy weekend when you don't feel like venturing out of the house? It's your problem now. And how soon before you're going to run out of clean shirts? Things you never had to think about before. But you'd better start thinking about them now.

Of course, single women have the same problems. And much of what's in this book applies equally to them. But this book is written for men. When couples are divorced or separated, it's usually the man who moves. Even if he doesn't, even if the wife moves and gives him back his closet, he's still suddenly wandering through uncharted territory. How the hell do you keep house?

According to popular mythology, single life is easier on the man. He moves around more freely while the woman is stuck at home (enjoying a better dinner than he does). He constantly meets new people. He cheerfully selects new partners as he bounces from bed to bed. His problem . . . *your problem* . . . is that on the mornings he wakes up alone, he doesn't know how to make the bed.

That's what this book is about. How to make a bed. How to find and furnish an apartment. How to equip a kitchen. Shop for food. Cook simple meals for one—or two. How to entertain your friends (or friend) or your children in your new home. And how to clean up the mess with the least amount of time and work.

Why do men need a book like this? Don't a lot of them take the practical approach and solve this problem by shacking up with an available woman? Yes, they do. But it's a mistake. A mistake for him. And a mistake for her.

Solving your housekeeping problems should not be your main motivation for a relationship with a woman. If you're a single man living alone for the first time, find out a little about how you like to live before you start playing house. If you're a man who's just come out of a broken marriage, you ought to give yourself time to sort out your feelings, to find out about women different from your wife, to avoid going into the same kind of mistake you just got out of. If you're a widower, you need time to adjust to the abrupt change in your status. For a woman, the disadvantages of "instant domesticity" are obvious. He wants her not because of the kind of person she is but because he's desperate for sleep-in help.

I start off with a couple of assumptions. One is that you left a home where there was a fairly well-defined division of labor. If you were married, you were the main, if not sole, breadwinner. If you're unmarried, you were in school or working. Whatever your status, women took care of the house. So you know zilch about running a household. Yes, even a single person's living quarters are a household!

My second assumption is that you've become accustomed to certain creature comforts. You now take them for granted and would like to maintain them. You like flaking out in a comfortable chair with your feet propped up on an ottoman and with a bowl of fresh fruit within easy reach. So buy a chair, buy an ottoman, buy a bowl, and buy some fruit. You like fresh flowers in the house. There is no recorded case of a florist refusing to sell a single man fresh-cut flowers for his apartment.

None of these chores was biologically assigned to the female of the species. A washing machine knob responds as well to a male's hand as to a female's. A butcher will as gladly sell lamb chops to a man as to a woman. You can learn to do it all by yourself. Look, women have entered the business world and have proven they can be at home any place except the men's room. Well, you can learn to run your home so well you'll make Mr. Clean look like a graduate of skid row. Even cooking. After all, despite all those colorful pictures of fluted vegetables found in the women's magazines, the best chefs are usually men.

I also assume you belong to that category called "middle income." If you're rich, your problems are minimal. I know money doesn't buy everything, but it can pay for a cleaning person, a decorator, a cook, good restaurants, entertainment, furniture from Knoll Associates. If that isn't everything, check with the guy rummaging around a Salvation Army warehouse for an armchair.

If you're poor—I mean really have no money, not just less than you had before—a lot of my advice will be meaningless. You won't be able to afford it.

And, lastly, I take for granted that you live in an urban or suburban area where goods and services are readily available. If you're stuck out on a farm twenty miles from the nearest supermarket, you may lead a horse to water, but you can't teach him to do the laundry.

I am going to discuss primarily practical problems. The "mechanics" of day-to-day living. I won't go too deeply into legal or emotional conflicts. If you are getting a divorce, no matter how amicable the separation, get your own lawyer and get a good one. Preferably one experienced in matrimonial matters. Divorce is a luxury for the rich. While it is true that you never know a person until you live with her, you've got a cornucopia of surprises in store for you when you try to "unlive" with her. A good lawyer can take care of a lot of unpleasant decisions you'd like to avoid. If you're just moving away from home for the first time, young man, it may be more than just mother's cooking you'll be missing.

And if you're deeply troubled, emotionally upset, not sleeping, wandering around the apartment until 3 A.M., don't rely on your friends' well-intentioned advice. Too often your married friends are busy plugging leaks in their own sinking marriage, in which case you can't be sure whether they're talking to you or themselves. If your problems persist, seek help from a psychologist or a psychiatrist. Your family doctor can help you find one. You're not out to save your marriage; you're out to save yourself. This may help keep you from repeating the same mistakes.

Read the advice in this book. You don't have to follow it to the letter. But you'll get plenty of ideas on how to work out living alone in a manner that best suits you. Once you get the hang of it (and that's easy) you'll discover that being suddenly single can suddenly be a hell of a lot of fun.

1

Can a Man Live Alone?
Don't Ask Your Mother

There was a time when everyone lived at home until he or she got married. After all, how could a single person, especially a man, ever learn to set up a household alone?

Before World War II, it was almost unthinkable to leave home while still unmarried. Why set up your own living quarters when your own folks had a "perfectly good bed for you to sleep in?" Only malcontents left the family bosom to strike out on their own. If you came from a good family, with a proper upbringing, you just didn't do that sort of thing. You waited until you got married, then had a woman to set up your own home.

Why marriage endows you with housekeeping instincts is beyond me. Of course, women were supposed to have absorbed a lot of domestic know-how by osmosis. But, men? They're helpless. They have to pair off with one of the osmotic sex and then they're allowed to set up their own households. It's like a conspiracy between the caterers and the real estate people.

A lot of this has changed today. Now it is common to go directly from college to your own apartment. Sometimes a person does it alone; more frequently he or she shares an apartment. It's not only people taking jobs away from home who set up housekeeping alone. Even young people who remain working in their hometowns now frequently move out and set up quarters. In fact, the people who remain home are now considered anachronisms. So today we have young men learning the occult arts of cooking, cleaning, and entertaining.

But this is a relatively new phenomenon. Most men over 35 followed the traditional path from family home to college, back to family, and then to marriage. When their marriages break up, they're stranded. They have no backlog of experience to draw on.

But it's experience that's easy to assimilate.

A friend of mine whom I'll call Gary (I'm going to use fictitious names throughout the book to protect men from women looking for sleep-in help) is 42. He came home one night to an empty apartment. His wife had fled, taking the children and his mother's recipe for chocolate cake.

Besides handling the emotional problems precipitated by the breakup of his marriage, Gary found it hard to cope with the routine of day-to-day living. Breakfast was easy. He would stop in at a luncheonette on his way to work. Sharing a counter with a group of strangers wasn't as relaxing as eating at his own kitchen table, and space for spreading out the morning paper was more cramped, but it was a solution, albeit not ideal, for getting early morning nourishment. Lunch, of course, was as before. And Gary usually ended his day with dinner at the corner hamburger joint. Not particularly festive, but when you're eating three meals a day in restaurants, even without a budget, all menus start to blur into a common pattern. The whole idea becomes less a meal to relax over than a nutritional chore to be dispensed with as quickly and as effortlessly as possible. Then Gary would end his day by heading home to attack a pile of dirty socks.

That's all in Gary's past now. He has moved into a new apartment. It's smaller, more suited to his actual needs, and it's cheaper. It isn't dusty with memories. He has decided that eating out is dreary and expensive.

Now, unless he is invited out, Gary cooks his own dinners at home. Nothing to make Julia Child jealous, but he is making himself good, simple meals. He occasionally invites dates up for dinner. He has even progressed to having a date and another couple up for dinner. And he's got his housekeeping down to a simple, manageable routine.

Look, nobody expects your apartment to be a candidate for a nine-page spread in *House Beautiful*. But your bachelor pad can be made pleasant and comfortable without a lot of fuss. Most people think the only thing a man can do around the house is move pianos. That's why they're surprised you haven't furnished in Early Army Barrack.

There's more than just personal comfort to be gained from setting up your own pad. Ladies are intrigued by a man who goes it alone. A guy holed up in a furnished room is an object of pity. That's great if you want to be mothered. But, hopefully, your relationships with women have progressed beyond such puerile role playing. Besides, a furnished room is not an idyllic setting for romance.

But, invite her to your own apartment and you fly your banner of independence. One look around at the comfortable furniture, the books, records, or whatever you own that expresses your own interests, and she reacts. Here's a guy with respect for himself. A guy who can handle his life himself. Here's a challenge. No mothering needed here. Besides sex, which is always a welcome house gift, what else can she offer? Herself as good company.

A guy who sets up his own apartment is really, in a sense, going along with the whole movement towards liberation of both sexes. He is saying that in today's world you don't assign tasks to people because of their sex. Housekeeping is not something demeaning for a man but okay for a woman. There are just certain jobs that have to be done in daily living by whoever picks up the dust cloth first.

Can a Man Live Alone? 7

Once you've learned how to fend for yourself, you find your mind a lot clearer about the women you become interested in. You are more likely to enjoy the woman for herself—as a human being and not just an easy solution to your housekeeping problems.

Too many men still cling to the old-fashioned male image of the helpless little boy around the house who is the master in bed. They try to solve their housekeeping dilemma by quickly shacking up with some woman. Since they don't give themselves breathing time between the breakup of their marriages and the start of new alliances, they unfortunately may make the same mistake in their choice of women.

There are some men who believe women were meant primarily for cleaning house and bedding down just as there are women who believe men were meant primarily for paying the bills. These people will hopefully all find each other and leave the rest of us alone.

Talk with guys who have separated from their wives. You'll find that they procrastinated about moving out because of the damned inconvenience of it all. Now they've got to start all over again and they don't know where to begin.

I know a lot of men who now live alone and like it. I'm not recommending the single life as the only way to live. That's a problem you'll have to solve on your own. But, as a single man setting up your own household, you enjoy a lot of advantages.

Chances are your home with your wife reflected her taste more than yours. Sure, you probably never gave much thought before to furniture. You met her at the store after she did all the shopping and merely nodded agreement to her choice of dining room chairs. If the price was right, you couldn't have cared less. You're going to be surprised at finding yourself a lot more comfortable with furnishings you've selected. The ashtrays will be more practical, the furniture more comfortable, the overall look less fussy.

And running your household will be a part-time job for you. You won't be able to give it the full day many women can. More and more women who hold jobs have had to reorganize their housekeeping chores because they have less time available. You can learn too. At best, housekeeping is an onerous chore with little reward. So you're going to approach it like a problem at work. How do you get it out of the way so you can get on with the next thing?

You'll find shortcuts, timesaving routines, your own needs, and patterns of work. Look, you handle your job efficiently, so why can't you apply the same techniques to running your house? You can.

My friend Danny went from 21 years of marriage to bachelorhood with all the ease of a skier traversing fresh powder snow. When Danny was married he never did a thing around the house. Nothing!

When he moved out, he first went to a hotel. After all, this was easiest. Besides, he couldn't conceive of even finding an apartment, much less housekeeping. But one month of having to get dressed to go downstairs for just a cup of coffee cured him of inadequacy. He searched for an apartment and found a comfortable three-room pad. First he bought a box spring and mattress and a coffeepot. He borrowed a card table and four folding chairs. Thus he could stand, lie down or sit in his own apartment. His sister-in-law helped him shop for furniture, although Danny retained the rights for final approval or veto. Gradually, Danny's apartment shaped into a comfortable home where he could invite his kids or friends. Once he solved the environment problem, Danny turned his attention to cooking. He started with boiling eggs and, bit by bit, expanded his culinary repertoire.

Today Danny entertains married friends for whom he whips up great dinners. His rewards are envious looks from the husbands and worried ones from the wives.

Chuck went through the same thing. From the time he was a little boy until the day he left home to be married, Chuck's mother picked up after him. She had what she considered a very clear sense of what women were supposed to do and what men were not supposed to do. And her analysis of role assignments gave her a lot of work and left Chuck without a care in the world.

Can a Man Live Alone?   9

It wasn't surprising that Chuck married a woman who continued his mother's approach to maintaining Chuck's creature comforts.

When his marriage broke up, Chuck did a very realistic about-face. Sure, it was great when somebody else kept the ashtrays empty and stocked the refrigerator with his favorite beer. But he knew immediately that, from now on, if he dropped a shirt on the floor it was going to stay there until he picked it up. So he picked it up because he found he liked all the neatness and comfort the women in his life had conspired to give him. He just had to start doing it himself. And he did.

If Danny and Chuck could make the transition, any man can. Even you. So let's learn how.

2
It's Your Apartment, Not Your Locker

The first thing you've got to do is find an apartment. Forget about male stoicism that claims that all you need is a place to hang your hat. You also need a place to hang your jacket and pants and a place to store your shirts. And you'll want to sit down occasionally.

If you are departing from the battle scene of a marriage, you may be willing to settle for housekeeping privileges in the back of a car. However, one of the purposes of your own pad is to give you a place in which to entertain women friends. That rules out the back of the car.

If you're a single man moving out from your parents' home, you are leaving an environment that they created to suit their needs and tastes. You may have been permitted some freedom within the confines of your own bedroom, but you had to keep those psyche-delic posters out of the rest of the house! With your own apartment, you can create your own life-style.

If you have children, you have to provide a place for them. You'll not only have them visiting you during the day, there will be times when they will stay over with you. Sometimes overnight; sometimes for a few nights. Where and how you live will have considerable influence on your children's attitudes towards you.

Also, as someone newly single, you will spend a lot of time alone. If you were used to the constant presence of others, being alone can, at least in the beginning, be very depressing. It's not made easier by shuffling around some rented room with an unobstructed view of the air shaft.

So you should try to find an apartment that's as decent as you can afford and furnish it comfortably. You'll find it will make the whole transition to single life easier. Plus it's a real ego trip when people express surprise that you're not living in a lean-to in which you've done clever things with orange crates.

Now to find an apartment. There are several sources. The most obvious is the real estate columns of your local paper. If you can, pick up the Sunday edition Saturday night. That gives you a few hours advantage over those who sleep late Sunday morning. If you live in a big city, there may be neighborhood papers which give you leads on apartments available in particular areas. For instance, in New York City *The Village Voice* lists many apartments that never get advertised in the more widely distributed *The New York Times*.

Check real estate brokers. Some confine themselves to circumscribed areas. Others will deal on a more city-wide basis. Brokers usually get a prearranged fee if they find something for you. Inquire about the fee arrangements when you speak with them. Contact the managing agents or real estate companies who manage apartment properties. You'll find them in the Yellow Pages. Or, just walk down the streets of any neighborhood that interests you. You'll usually find the managing agents' names posted on the exteriors of the buildings. If not, ask superintendents.

Superintendents often act as renting agents for buildings. In any case, they often know of vacancies coming up in their buildings that have not yet been listed as available. Sometimes, walking the streets rewards you with a "Vacancy" sign that's newly posted. And, of course, tell everyone you know—friends, relatives, fellow workers—that you're looking. In other words, exploit every available source.

Before you launch the search, you must ask yourself a couple of questions. First (and most obvious), how much rent can you afford? Second, how much room do you need?

A couple of other things to bear in mind. Do you have a strong preference for a particular neighborhood? In small towns this is not important, but in cities neighborhoods take on characteristics. Does that local flavor reflect your life-style? You should try to find out. If the area is popular with young swingers and you're over 45, don't move in and invite a cardiac arrest.

A friend of mine whose adolescence had long since passed moved into a building stocked with airline hostesses, nubile secretaries and other delicacies. He had been a quiet family man who was one of Kinsey's less interesting statistics. In his new apartment he was constantly being badgered for ice, liquor, cigarettes. Parties often erupted into the public halls. Eventually he found living in a residential singles bar too taxing. He moved.

Are there parks or playgrounds nearby? In spring, summer or fall, the advantages of a nearby park are obvious. It's a nice place to sit and read the paper. It's a nice place to meet people. If you have small children, playgrounds need no explanation. Is there playground equipment? Is it in reasonably good condition? If you have small children, check for rubber safety pads under swings.

You should also check the neighborhood for shopping conveniences. Is there a laundromat nearby (in case your building doesn't have a laundry room that's kept open at night)? You don't have to sit there in the laundromat. Many will take your soiled laundry and return it to you clean a few hours later. Is there a supermarket? How late is it open? A dry cleaner? A drugstore? A hardware store? A shoemaker? A liquor store? A newsstand or stationery store? The more of these conveniences available in your immediate neighborhood, the easier life becomes.

Item Number One: the rent. There's no need for a long discussion here. You should know how much you can afford. However, many items influence how much rent you can actually pay. For instance, does the rent include gas and electricity? Is there a broker's fee? That's extra and can be amortized over your lease. Transportation costs to and from work can be rationalized as part of your rent. If you can walk to work, you can afford to pay a little more rent. Of course, you can eliminate the entire transportation expense by a single outlay for a bicycle. Once you own it, transportation is gratis, pollution-free, and guaranteed to save your waistline as well as money.

Item Number Two: space. Do you have children who will visit with you? You've got to provide room for them to sleep over. Do you do work at home that requires more than just desk space? Do you have a space-consuming hobby that you plan to continue? Are you bringing any furniture with you from your former home? If they are big pieces, measure doors to see if you can move them in. Measure walls to make sure they'll fit.

Try to find at least a three-room apartment: living room, bedroom, kitchen, and bath. A foyer large enough for dining is a bonus. If you are financially restricted to a studio (no bedroom), try to find one with a sleeping alcove or a dining alcove or foyer that can be used for sleeping. You might find it confining to do all your living within the same four walls. If you're moving out of a large house or are physically a big person, tiny quarters can make you positively claustrophobic.

There are a few things you should look for. Try to find a place with windows facing south and/or west. A southern exposure assures you cheering sunshine. Most of the prevailing breezes come from the west. Whichever way the windows face, find out if you have to supply shades. Are there any broken panes that need replacing? Check the windows for tight closing. Do any of them show signs of water damage from rain leaking through? Do any open onto a fire escape or other access? Beware of windows that are two vertical sections held in place by a common turn-latch. A burglar can easily slide a knife blade in between the two sections of the window, flip the latch out of its cradle and push open the window. Can you install an iron grill or other safety device?

Don't neglect the kitchen. Right now you might be willing to settle for the corner pizza joint or TV dinners. You'll get over that. At least your stomach will. You might not believe it now but eventually you'll be entertaining in your own apartment. Unless you've got a fat wallet, you'll find constantly taking women out to dinner prohibitively expensive. You'll be forced into the kitchen by sheer economics. And even if *she* offers to make dinner at your place, she's got to have a place to cook.

So check the condition of the kitchen appliances. Do all the burners on the range work? The oven? Does the oven look as if someone is still saving grease from World War II? Ask the superintendent to have it cleaned. (There's no guarantee he'll comply but you'll never know unless you ask.) Is the oven door loose? Check the faucets in the sink. Do they drip? Do they release sufficient pressure? Do the cabinet doors close firmly? Are any handles missing? Any shelves missing or broken?

Does the refrigerator door close firmly? Any shelves missing? Ice cube trays missing? Is the inside of the refrigerator permanently soiled? Check underneath for roach-luring dirt. Is the insulation around the door intact or is it deteriorating? Is there counter work space? If there is little counter space, is there room for a small table and chair or for a wall-hung counter and stool? Yes, you can manage without them, but they are a great convenience if you have the room. It's easier for breakfast and lunch than setting up in your dining area. Are there drawers for utensils and other kitchen paraphernalia? Does the floor need retiling?

Check the closet space. The more the better. Are the rods and overhead shelves in place? One advantage of extra closet space is that you can store off-season clothes at home instead of paying the dry cleaner for this service. Do the closet doors close tightly or have too many layers of paint made this a memory? If any of the closets have a mirror hung on the door, check to see if it's cracked.

Is there a broom closet? If not, where can you store cleaning equipment like the vacuum cleaner, mop, bucket, etc.? Don't be misled by a couple of empty closets. Closets fill up quickly. Find out if there is public storage space in the basement. Many apartment houses provide some. It's a convenient place to store luggage, skis, bicycles. Check on how safe it is. Can you store a locked trunk or locker there? Is it kept locked? Who has the keys?

Can all the tenants enter and leave without supervision? Is it easy for outside delivery people or strangers to gain access to it? People have had chained bicycles stolen from common storage rooms. Will your household insurance cover items stored there? Sometimes, but rarely, buildings assign storage bins to each tenant. This, of course, is the safest and most convenient.

If there's a fireplace, does it work? If it does, and you plan to use it, have the flue cleaned out as soon as possible. This will improve the draw. There are professionals who provide this service. If you live in a city, be prepared to pay dearly for firewood. You might settle for just making a fire with your wallet. It won't burn as long, but it could be cheaper.

If the apartment needs a lot of work, decide how much the landlord will do, how much you will have to do, and how much you're going to have to pay other people to do. Superintendents can be very helpful here. Their cooperation grows in direct proportion to the money used to fertilize it. This often turns out to be a cheaper way of getting things done. If he has a handyman on staff who's being paid anyway, he can divert his workload to your apartment. The super often knows service people in the neighborhood. He may know of a good, not-too-expensive carpenter. If you're a do-it-yourselfer, you've got happy times ahead. Personally, I'm as prehensile as the next guy, but I've got recessive carpentry genes.

There are some other things to check. Is the apartment air-conditioned? If you are buying units from a previous tenant, have them checked before you pay for them. If there is no air conditioning, is the building wired for it? If not, must you pay for the wiring? If you're on an upper floor, this can be a big item. If electricity is included in your rent, is there an extra monthly charge for the use of the unit? Air conditioning is important unless you live in an area where you just divorced a penguin.

Do you have to paint the apartment yourself? Does your lease state the landlord's obligation about initial painting and subsequent repaintings? Is there wallpaper that needs removing? Do the wooden floors need rescraping?

How's the soundproofing in the building? The soft gurgling of your neighbor's toilet is not reminiscent of a mountain stream. Are there a lot of traffic noises? If you're a light sleeper but you like the apartment, decide you'll get used to it or sleep with ear plugs.

Check the general appearance of the building. Are the halls and lobby reasonably clean? Is there an incinerator drop on each floor? If not, is there a schedule for garbage pickup, or do you have to drop it off someplace yourself? If so, are cans always available? There shouldn't be any hassle unless your landlord is trying to circumvent the local health code. He has to make adequate provisions.

Unfortunately, most apartment buildings in cities have non-paying residents: roaches. They come in with grocery deliveries. They flourish in areas where people are careless about garbage or uncovered food. Ask the super to have the apartment checked by an exterminator before you move in. Very often local health laws govern your rights in this area. The City Health Department can advise you.

Does the building show telltale signs of little children? At the risk of sounding anti-children, I suggest you consider whether you want to be in a building with lots of little ones racing up and down the halls. Yeah, I know they're not supposed to, but many parents seeking peace and quiet achieve it by letting you share their children. Of course, if you have small children who will be visiting, this built-in playmate facility can be a plus.

Get a lease. What are your sublet rights? Legal restrictions? How many people can occupy the apartment? Must they be related to you? If you don't understand leases, have a lawyer check yours.

Okay. You found an apartment. Now what do you do first?

Painting and Repairs

Try to get as much of the basic work done as you can before you move in. Floor scraping, if needed. Painting. Repairing closets, plumbing, cabinets, appliances. You'll find plenty more to be done after you move in.

The most basic is the painting, even if you're going to do it yourself. Yes, it can be done after you've moved in. It's just a lot easier to paint when you don't have to move any furniture, clothes or other things. With that first paint job, try to do the inside of all the closets and cabinets too. Once you've done these interiors, you can forget about doing them again for years.

Don't get hung up on a color chart unless you're going all out and doing an entire apartment—furniture, rugs, lamps: the works—all in one fell swoop. If you're like most people, you'll do it piecemeal, as time and money permit. When in doubt, paint white or, preferably, off-white. White reflects the most light, which is a point to keep in mind if your apartment gets little natural light.

If you pick a color, choose one you like and not one someone else insists you should have. Let that one color predominate throughout the apartment, in paint, furnishings, etc. A lot of different colors create a very busy look. One color, even with variations, will create a more restful look. So decide what kind of environment you want to live in.

Use flat paint in all the rooms except the kitchen and bathroom. In these use a semi-gloss. These rooms get a lot of abuse and semi-gloss paint can be wiped clean.

Window Shades and Blinds

After painting, the next thing you want to do is cover the windows. If the apartment comes with blinds or shades, you've skipped this problem. But suppose it doesn't. You need shades, blinds or shutters for privacy, depending on your commitment to exhibitionism. You also need them to keep out light when you're sleeping and to keep out the summer sun on hot days.

The most common blinds are Venetian blinds, in which slats lie horizontally. A newer type of blind is one in which the slats are inserted vertically. The problem with Venetian blinds is that they are terrible dust collectors. They just get plain dirty and have to be wiped clean. Their advantage is that you can regulate the amount of light you want without completely closing off the outside as you do with shades. Vertical blinds turn 180 degrees to let in light. They roll up like shades.

Shades can be fabric, plastic, woven wood, or split bamboo. Prices vary from very cheap for plain plastic or cotton to very expensive for elaborate Roman shades that are raised in an accordion-pleat and are usually made of expensive fabric. One good idea for your bedroom is night shades. These are laminated, the middle layer being a dark fabric, which is the most effective shade for keeping out light. The outer fabric can be a plain color or, if you want, a printed fabric. The plainer the cheaper.

Split bamboo shades are natural color and usually roll up. You can have them installed to pull across as a traverse curtain. Woven wood can also be installed as either a roll-up shade or a traverse curtain. Split bamboo is very informal looking, and moderately effective as a light obstruction. Woven wood is very modern looking.

Shutters can be bought unpainted or completely finished. You can have them installed by the supplier or do it yourself if you want to brush up on your cursing. Shutters also collect dust.

Floorings

If you're lucky you won't have to retile the bathroom or kitchen. Bathrooms usually come with ceramic tile already installed. It's the kitchen that often needs redoing. Maybe the landlord will do it for you. If you have to have it done yourself, there are several materials available. Linoleum comes in several types, including probably the most inexpensive floor covering you can get. Piece linoleum is cheap and easy to install. Asphalt tile is also inexpensive. It comes in both individual squares and rolls. Rubber tile is soft underfoot and quiet but more expensive. Cork, available both in squares and strips, is very good looking but also more costly. It is not like bulletin-board cork. It has a hard, smooth finish.

Vinyl asbestos is medium priced and durable. Pure vinyl costs more but it is extremely durable. Vinyls now come in a high polish finish which never needs waxing. You just wash it clean and the high gloss returns. You can also buy washable outdoor carpeting for the bathroom and/or kitchen.

As long as you're into flooring, you might consider tiling the entry foyer and the dining area. These areas get a lot of abuse and tiling is easier to maintain.

A Bed Is for Sleeping

Now you've got to furnish. All you absolutely must have to start is a bed to sleep in. Borrow a card table and four chairs for eating and sitting. Buy a kitchen step stool for reaching. Open packing cases, such as movers use, can be stacked on their sides, open side out, for storage of clothes and linen until you decide what kind of permanent storage units you want. Just line them with the tissue paper that cleaners stuff into your coat sleeves.

About that bed. If you're in a studio apartment, your bed will doubtless serve as a sofa. Or you may buy one of those overstuffed armchairs that open out to a bed. This is a less satisfactory arrangement, best only for occasional use. You should get something that can serve as a real bed for the most comfortable sleeping.

You have several options open to you. The first is a three-quarter box spring and mattress shoved into a corner or against a wall for back support. Cover it with a throw and small pillows or bolsters and you're in business. Your next choice is one or, if you have the room, two single-size box springs and mattresses. This gives you two sofas plus extra sleeping space. Depending on your wall space, they can be lined up in tandem, placed at right angles to one another in a corner, or placed opposite each other across a room.

You could also buy a sofa that opens up into a bed. These are widely available in department stores, furniture stores, and manufacturers' retail outlets. An inexpensive solution is a wooden platform on legs on which you place a mattress. There are also platform bases available with storage units built underneath. This is an especially practical solution if you're in a small apartment that lacks storage space for blankets, pillows, or extra bed linen.

Another option is the trundle bed. A trundle bed is a single bed with a second single bed which slides out from underneath and rises to conventional height. This is a space-saving answer to a need for additional sleeping space, such as when friends or children sleep over.

Then, of course, for desperately cramped quarters there is the murphy bed. This is a platform and mattress on a hinge that folds up against the wall when not in use. It's more trouble because you'll probably have to have it made to order.

A bedroom, of course, allows you to just buy a regular bed.

As a general rule, I would advise against twin beds. Twin beds make it difficult to refuse guests you would rather not put up. Like a relative who pops into town unexpectedly for an overnight visit. Or a male friend who works late and misses the last train back to the suburbs. With a double, queen-sized, or king-sized bed you choose your own guests. Anyone who accepts your hospitality knows what the sleeping arrangements are.

Perhaps I'm bringing up sex a little too soon. While young single men away from home for the first time are panting to get their own sleeping quarters, many men who move out on a marriage, or whose wives die, shun carnal pleasures for a while. In fact, some even discover that their virile powers seem to have deserted them. This, fortunately, passes with time. Eventually, anything that's down must come up. So buy a bed with anticipation.

In a bedroom too, you have options. You can get a box spring with mattress. You can choose any of the options recommended for a studio apartment.

There are several kinds of mattresses available: foam, hair, felt, built-in innersprings, and combinations. The mattress is the wrong place to economize. Get the best you can afford. A firm mattress generally means better support and, therefore, more restful sleep.

The bedding department of a department store will be able to point out to you how the various types of fillings differ. Check the classified section of the telephone book for other sources.

A new kind of sleeping equipment to come onto the scene is the waterbed. A waterbed, in case you're not up on the latest marine information, is a rubberized casing or vinyl bag filled with water.

They range from single to king (or admiral) size. If you have never lain on a waterbed, let me assure you it is a surprisingly pleasant sensation. Plopping onto a waterbed is like falling into the middle of a rhythm lesson. Some find it a comforting return to the placental sac. Aficionados swear by its orthopedic effects; they claim it is the most comfortable, body-supporting bed they have ever slept in.

When you buy a waterbed you actually get a bag and an easily assembled frame into or onto which the bag fits. The store from which you buy the bed will loan you a pump which you attach to an ordinary sink faucet in order to get the bed afloat. Good waterbeds come with heating units which keep the water at a comfortable temperature. Otherwise the water would be too cold to sleep on; your body heat escapes into the water. The temperature problem with cheaper beds which have no heating unit is solved by placing an insulating pad, such as foam rubber, over the mattress. You can also buy a heater which fits under the bag and maintains the water at a lovely 92 degrees. It's the Caribbean right in your own bedroom.

If you buy a waterbed, let me caution you about a couple of points. First, a filled full-size waterbed weighs several hundred pounds. Be sure your floors are strong enough to support this weight. Also, be absolutely certain about where you want the bed placed. Once it's filled you're not about to start moving this trapped ocean around. Finally, be sure any heating elements you buy are approved by the Underwriters' Laboratories.

Pillows, too, come in a variety of fillings and sizes. This is a matter of personal preference. All down is the softest. Many pillow manufacturers recommend a combination of down and feathers for greater firmness. You can buy pillows stuffed with foam, synthetic fibers, or all feathers. You can also select non-allergenic fillings. Pillows also come in sizes. You can get big, king-sized pillows for big, king-sized heads. Buy at least one extra pillow for a guest.

You don't have to go right out and buy a bed for your mattress. If you're unsure of what kind of base you want, just buy the mattress. Spread a sheet on the floor, place the mattress on top of it

and go to sleep while you decide how you're going to furnish.
Now for the real furniture.

Selecting Furniture

There are three basic approaches to decorating an apartment.
The first is "do-it-yourself." The second is to call in friends and
relatives who have some knowledge of decorating or whose taste
you respect. The third, and most expensive (though usually the
best), is to hire a decorator.

"Do-it-yourself" is not recommended for most men because of
their general lack of interest or experience in home furnishings.
However, if you combine this with assistance from knowledgeable
friends, you might make a go of it. Decorators usually buy furniture
wholesale and then charge you a percentage above the wholesale
price. Some decorators work on an hourly basis. This is an excellent solution. You can use the decorator's services merely to help
you select major pieces of furniture or to give you some general
advice on how to go about furnishing your pad. Some department
stores maintain decorator services which will be glad to work with
you. It's assumed you will buy your furniture at their store.

A decorator saves you the most tedious part of buying furniture:
the shopping. Once he has determined your taste, he can supply
you with pictures similar to your preference. All you've got to do
is look at them and nod approval or rejection. Whatever you do, be
firm about choosing only things *you* like. Someone else may try
to convince you that a piece of furniture is smashing, but once
you get it home that's exactly what you might feel like doing with it.

Whichever route you take—alone, with friends, or with a decorator—the first thing you should do is make a rough floorplan
of your apartment. Measure the length and height of the walls.
Indicate the placement of doors and windows. This will be an indis-
pensable guide in figuring out the size of the furniture pieces you
can fit into your apartment. You can't place an eight-foot sofa
against a five-foot wall.

Obviously, the less money you have, the more you must substitute ingenuity. Those men with money will easily find their way. They'll end up with a decorator or in a good furniture store and they'll write checks. The problems loom larger for those with little or no money. And for most men it looms.

There are several sources for inexpensive furniture. The first and most obvious is anything you bring from your former home. The second is castaway pieces gathering dust in relatives' or friends' attics. These are treasures that can easily be freshened. A coat of paint or varnish, a little lubricant on the drawer slides, a couple of broken drawer knobs replaced, a slipcover to hide worn or faded upholstery.

After foraging the attics, your next choice is the Salvation Army or Thrift Shops. Don't turn your nose up at these. A lot of people give darned good furniture to these outlets. Maybe they had no one to give it to. Or perhaps they tried to sell it but couldn't and would just as soon enjoy the tax deduction of a donation to a charity. You may have to do some refinishing or reupholstering.

Classified ads in newspapers often offer secondhand furniture. Don't cringe at the idea of "secondhand." All antique furniture is secondhand. Some cities have newspapers which specialize in merchandise offerings. For instance, in New York City *Buy Lines* is a constant source of leads to used furniture. Inquire at newsstands in your own town to see if there are local papers of this sort available.

For the financially desperate there is one last route. And don't be embarrassed. You won't be the first person to try this. Nor will you be the last. Some people have furnished with discards they have found on the streets: old pieces people have put out for the garbage collector. It may be any old over-stuffed chair which is no longer so over-stuffed. So just restuff it, clean it off and throw a cotton cloth over it until you can buy better. Be careful such discarded items are not occupied by fleas or bedbugs. Perhaps it's a small table or chair with a rung or leg missing. You can buy legs at furniture yards or stores. And if it's a lamp that just needs a new shade and some rewiring, let there be light!

In some cities lumberyards, hardware stores, and even some department stores carry good-looking, simple furniture-in-the-raw.

This means unpainted chests, chairs, tables, bed and sofa bases that merely need a coat of paint or varnish or—for fast decorating —a layer of contact paper. The furniture is usually assembled, though some places sell kits. These include all the parts, which you then assemble yourself. You're not competing with the Blue Room at the White House, but you are saving money.

How much furniture you need naturally depends on the size of your apartment. If you have rooms that serve separate functions, obviously you buy furniture for each room. If, however, you have smaller quarters, much of your furniture will have to serve double duty. Chairs can double for lounging and dining. A chest can pinch-hit as a table base for a tabletop that is kept stored in a closet. Whatever you do, don't overload the place. It's just that much more to clean.

There are a few basics to keep in mind. Try to budget yourself for at least one good comfortable chair to lounge in. If it's got an ottoman on which to prop your weary feet, you may never miss your wife.

There is an inexhaustible supply of good ideas for chairs. One of the most common is the director's chair, an extremely comfortable chair for sitting, lounging or dining. It is a folding chair with arm rests, one sling for back support, and another for the seat. They are available from many sources: outdoor furniture stores, department stores, furniture stores, mail order houses. They are inexpensive enough for you to order a couple of extras to store in a closet and pull out for emergency seating. The slings can be canvas, fabric, leather, fur, vinyl—almost anything that can be sewn into a sling. This also means you can choose from a wide range of colors for the slings. If you plan to use director's chairs for dining or desk work, keep in mind that they run a bit lower in height than most chairs. Therefore, you'll have to accommodate your table height to the lower level of the chair.

There are also other types of folding or collapsible chairs available. Some come with rush or rattan seating. In the last few years inflatable furniture has appeared. And more recently a shapeless bean bag has come onto the market. You just plop into it and the filling adjusts to your contours better than your clothes do. You can also find inexpensive wicker or molded plastic. Your choice is endless.

Don't just look at the chair. Sit in it to see if it's comfortable. Is it sturdy? If it wobbles when brand new, it won't get any steadier with use.

You need a table at which to eat. Buy one that seats at least two comfortably but can be opened up to accommodate four to six. It'll hold more for poker. You don't have to buy four dining chairs. You can manage with two plus a couple of folding chairs stored in a closet. Of course, if you have a separate dining area with enough room, then buy four chairs.

A dining table does not have to be expensive. You can buy a base or legs and top separately. The top can be a veneered wood, laminated plastic, glass, solid wood, marble, slate or butcher block. Match the top to your taste and pocket. Naturally, some of these tops are absolutely carefree. You just wipe them clean after eating.

You can also buy a secondhand desk which comes fitted with a single level of thin drawers, leaving you plenty of leg room on all four sides. If it doubles as a desk, store stationery supplies in the drawers. If not, keep coasters, trivets and silverware in them.

If you are terribly cramped for space, you can hinge a table top to the wall and lower it when you need to. Or store a plank behind the sofa and a couple of sawhorses in the closet. Drag the whole thing out when you have to seat more than yourself. Leafing through magazines and shopping furniture stores will give you other ideas about tables as well as other pieces of furniture.

Buy some kind of sofa, even if it's just for yourself to stretch out on. Sofas can run high, but you can easily settle for a foam rubber pad and bolsters on a platform.

A coffee table gives you a place to drop the mail and place an ashtray and a drink. The same information given for a dining table applies to coffee tables. You can even use an old crate and cover it with contact paper or plastic material. Or a plank of wood on a couple of low sawhorses or other comparable support.

How many chests do you need? It depends on the size of your wardrobe. You can eliminate some of the need if your closets are large enough to accommodate a tier of shelves for clothing or linen. Just remember that men's clothing tends to be bulky, so be sure the drawers are deep enough to hold shirts and sweaters. Very bulky sweaters can be stored on closet shelves.

One idea you can use for chest storage is to buy secondhand office files two or three drawers deep. Place a board over them and you've got storage plus a dresser top or a desk. This arrangement also works in the living room or foyer. It can be especially useful if the apartment does not come with a linen closet and you have to find some place to store these items.

I assume you brought your tie rack with you. If your wife has taken up with another guy, let him get his own tie rack. If there is no full-length mirror in the bedroom, install one. You never know when someone might want to check her hemline.

A chair in the bedroom is great for propping your feet when tying a shoelace. It is also a convenient holder for the bedspread at night. Pick a chair that can double as a dining chair.

Bookcases can be as simple as 2-by-4-inch pine planks supported on bricks or as elaborate as custom-designed wall systems. There's plenty in between. You can buy knock-down bookshelves you assemble yourself. You can buy ready-made bookshelves from single shelves to as many as you like. Standards and brackets give you flexibility of space between the shelves. There are all kinds of wall strips and poles from which you hang shelves, cabinets, lights. They reach up to the ceiling and give a custom built-in look to the installation. And, of course, you can stack wooden crates, connect them with corrugated nails and fill as desired.

You are going to need some extra tables around. Here, too, you have a lot to choose from. One variation is wooden cubes which have one open side. The top can be used as a table surface next to a chair. The open space becomes storage for records or magazines.

Let There Be Light

Pick your lamps for lighting, not decorating. You should place one next to any chair or sofa where you intend to read. At least one lamp in the living room should have a 3-way bulb to give general illumination to the room. You may not like what you see, but with good light at least you won't bump into it. Spotlights can be attached to walls or hung from ceilings. There is a wide variety of paper, plastic, parchment or glass globes available. These give good diffused lighting. If you hook them up with a dimmer switch, you vary all the way from mood lighting to "Look, Ma, I'm dancing!" A simple wall spotlight over the bed instead of a more expensive, elaborate lamp can suffice for reading. There are flexible Swedish lamps that can be raised, lowered, extended and pivoted. They come with metal shades in chrome or in a selection of painted colors.

Dependable as your lamps are, keep a flashlight and a package of candles handy in case of a power failure.

A recent trend in furniture stores has been the specialty stores that feature a wide selection of inexpensive lamps and furnishings. Most of it is modern; some, period. A lot of it is copied from expensive high-style design. In most large cities you will find this type of store catering to people searching for inexpensive but good-looking furnishings.

You'll have to fill in with ashtrays, an alarm clock or clock radio for the bedroom, a TV set, a waste basket in the bathroom and kitchen plus one near the desk or somewhere in the living room area. The need for other incidental items will crop up as you need them.

Rugs and Carpets

Floor coverings in kitchens and bathrooms should be washable. Stores now sell bathroom carpeting, which is another thing to clean. A good sized bathmat should suffice. Don't go to the expense of wall-to-wall carpeting in the other rooms unless the floors are in such bad condition you're ashamed to let your mother see them. If the floors are in reasonably good shape, just give them a good waxing and buy room-size or area rugs. There are professionals who will do your floors a lot better than you can. Their polishing equipment is heavier, which is an important factor in applying wax. You can, however, rent floor polishing equipment and do the job yourself. It's cheaper but more work.

One rug is a necessity alongside the bed. You don't need the Spartan experience of awakening in the morning and setting your feet on a cold floor. And your downstairs neighbor doesn't need to hear you dropping your shoes. Your need for rugs in other rooms will be dictated by placement of the furniture.

Rugs come in a variety of materials: cotton, wool, synthetics, and blends of any of these. Cotton is generally inexpensive and comes in a great range of vibrant colors. Synthetics also run the gamut of colors. Wool is still considered the finest material for rugs. It cleans well, wears well, feels great underfoot. Rugs, of course, come in solids as well as patterns. Patterns include a variety of handcrafted rugs such as those that come from Mexico, Morocco, Spain and Portugal. And there are Orientals from China and the Near East. A type of rug that is very popular is the shag rug. Some of them come with piles that are so long you can get lost in them. Shag rugs are hard to clean, but everything sifts down into the pile anyway so you don't have to bother. However, there are now vacuum machines equipped especially to clean shags.

Another thing you may not want to bother with is curtains or drapes. One of the advantages of colored or printed window shades is that they often supply the decorative touch people try to get with drapes. With rooms done in period style, drapes or curtains are often needed to finish off the room as well as your wallet.

Household Linen

You will also need household linen: bed linen, table linen and towels. If your breakaway occurs in January or May, you have fortuitously timed it with the semi-annual white sales staged by all the major department stores. Linens, towels, blankets, pillows are all marked down. While this can save you money, I don't think it's enough to make you postpone splitting to your own place.

Sheets and mattress pads are sized according to the size of your mattress; pillowcases, to the size of your pillow. A mattress pad protects the mattress and keeps it clean. Incidentally, it's a good idea to turn your mattress every few months. This distributes the wear more evenly over the surface.

Sheets and pillowcases come in percale, muslin, or a combination of polyester and cotton. You can also get all-synthetic, such as nylon. Exotic materials like silk or satin are also available for those of you who need all the help you can get. Muslin is the cheapest and comes in several grades. They are coarser than percale. Percale is not only smoother to the feel, it is more durable and, naturally, more expensive. Percale, too, comes in several grades. The higher the thread count (read the labels), the finer the sheet.

Polyester and cotton sheets and pillowcases need little or no ironing. They can be washed in a washing machine. This saves you laundry bills. Their disadvantage is that, like all-synthetic linen, they are less absorbent than all-cotton. They can feel clammy if you perspire in bed, particularly on warm summer nights.

Fitted bottom sheets, though slightly more expensive, simplify bed making. There are no corners to tuck in. The sheets also remain smooth and taut. Top sheets need not be fitted. You can use conventional sheets and just fold the corners in under the mattress. *Buy at least three sets of sheets and pillowcases.* That's one set on the bed, one in the laundry, and one to spare.

You need two types of blankets: heavy ones for winter, light ones for summer. As a general rule, the heavier the blanket, the warmer it is. Acrylic and wool blankets are the warmest. For summer, look into lightweight thermal blankets or cotton quilts. Electric blankets are lightweight and can be regulated to desired warmth. If you use an electric blanket, take advantage of its purpose and pre-heat the bed before you hop in.

In the last few years household linens have undergone a design revolution. There was a time when all bed linen was white. Solid colors started appearing many years ago. Now bed linen has been attacked by designers with abstract patterns, brilliant colors, wildly imaginative designs. Today even just plain going to sleep can be fun.

This should finally get us out of bed.

Now the bathroom. You need bath towels. Be good to yourself. Get generous size bath towels. You also need face towels and wash cloths. These can all be bought in sets or singly. *Buy at least a half dozen bath towels, a half dozen face towels, and three or four wash cloths. Also buy a couple of terry bath mats for the floor.* While you're in this department, pick up a couple of small terry hand towels for guests. If you have a tub/shower, buy a non-skid rubber mat. You can also buy non-skid strips that adhere to the bottom of the tub. You need some kind of a towel rack if one isn't built in. A drying rod for laundry doesn't have to be one of those complicated folding contraptions that take up the whole tub. There are modern fold-away or collapsible wall units that are much more convenient. If there is no built-in laundry hamper, buy one. A basket with a cover will do. Pick up a half dozen dish towels. The best choice is terry cloth. It's highly absorbent, needs no ironing and wears well. You can always use paper towels. It saves laundry.

For table linen you need only a few place mats. Cork or woven plastic simply wipes clean. There are also some heavy woven cloth ones which can be washed without ironing. An excellent choice for place mats is terry hand towels. Buy just a few napkins to match some of the mats. This is for company. Generally you'll use paper napkins.

Pictures on the Walls and Other Dust Collectors

Decorating details, such as pictures, are purely personal. But there is a wide range of expression open to you. You don't have to stick to Millet's "The Angelus."

If you are already an art buff then you know that good prints of your favorite artists don't have to be expensive. Museum stores are one good source for prints. Frame shops, art supply houses, and department stores also offer good reproductions.

Art exhibition posters are bright, cheerful, well-designed, and inexpensive. Travel posters are free. You can pick them up at airline offices and at travel information centers of foreign countries. If you're a photography bug, decorate the walls with prints of your own work. Some people use the finger paintings and crayon scrawls of their small children. This is the cheapest and the supply is inexhaustible. If you do this, please don't insist that people make some intelligent comment on your child's unintelligible scribbles. Just be content with the fact that you like it or that it's covering up a crack in the plaster.

You don't have to spend a lot of money for frames. First, you often find old frames in secondhand shops. Also, art supply houses, department stores and museums now carry framing kits. You select the size you need and quickly assemble the frame yourself. Over-sized pieces, like travel posters, can just be tacked to the wall or hung with a poster no-frame—two pieces of plastic applied to each end of the poster.

There are many other decorative touches depending on your pocketbook, the amount of time you're willing to put into the search and your particular interests. Wall hangings are one. They can be as simple as a piece of printed, batik-dyed or tie-dyed fabric or as elaborate as an old tapestry. Hang a small rug on the wall. It doesn't have to be an expensive Navajo blanket. It can be a Mexican copy of Navajo designs. There are Scandinavian Rya rugs that give you good design for wall hangings.

Check out antique or just plain junk shops. You can find over-sized letters or numerals of brass or gilt-painted wood. Old wooden printing blocks or tools are very handsome.

If you're a wine buff, stack your wine racks against the wall. If you're a food buff and have any money left for eating out in good restaurants, make a montage of the menus for a wall decoration.

Then there is the area of oversized graphics which you paint right on the wall. A painted arrow that runs across the wall and up onto the ceiling. Or some other design of bright colors that travels along from wall to the next and then zigzags down into a corner. This is highly individualistic, startling, modern and darned difficult to do. But it's your place, and if this strikes you as fun, try it. You can always paint over it. If you don't want to paint, you can make designs with contact paper.

Some men who found gardening relaxing while living at home transfer that interest to house plants. One widower who had a small greenhouse moved into a sunny apartment. He started with potted plants. Now he has a couple of terrariums in which he raises more exotic plant species. Another single man has made two large fish tanks the focal point of his living room. Beware of a hobby that ties you to the apartment when you would prefer to go away. Baby-sitting arrangements for a school of unappreciative fish or plants which need daily care is a bother and could be expensive. Plants survive well over a few days by first being watered thoroughly, then wrapped in plastic dry-cleaning bags. Punch a few holes in the bags to allow for ventilation.

Visit one of the local "head" shops. They feature psychedelic lighting features and other gimmickery that'll update your image while it aggravates your astigmatism.

These are details you can handle once you have put the major work behind you. Just keep in mind that your apartment is not a showplace for friends and neighbors. Its main purpose is to provide comfort for you.

Getting the Most Storage Space

Once you've assembled your major furniture and start settling in, you'll find you're suffering from a common ailment that afflicts apartment dwellers: lack of storage space. If you're fortunate enough to move into an old building, chances are the closets will be a decent size. In newer buildings, closets seem to be designed for people with two sets of clothes—one they're wearing, the other hangs in the closet. A basic conflict in American society is that the economy tries to get us to buy more goods, but the builders don't give us any place to store them. However, even the smallest apartment can be improved with space-saving storage ideas.

One of the most obvious is to build or place in a closet a tier of shelves. If it's a deep closet, you can place it in the back for storing things you rarely go to but haven't decided to throw out yet. A narrow tier towards the front can hold frequently used items, like hats, sweaters, gloves.

Closet shops in department stores sell small inexpensive cardboard or plywood chests of drawers that fit into a closet. Hang a large French bread basket on angle screws on the inside of your coat closet. It's a perfect receptacle for gloves and mufflers. Shoe bags can be used to store more than shoes. They hold tools, extension cords, cleaning brushes, and rags.

If you have to keep your bicycle in your apartment, put a heavy hook into the ceiling and hang the bike from it. It gets it off the floor. Or you could buy a folding bike that would fit in a closet.

You can build an inexpensive storage unit using file cabinets and stacked wooden cubes with one open side. An old trunk can double for storage and as a tabletop. An inexpensive foot locker does the same thing. If you don't like its looks, paint it a bright color or cover it with contact paper. Some old trunks become handsome pieces of furniture. Wicker baskets range from picnic hampers to trunk size. They're good looking, cheap, and can double as side tables.

A pegboard wall in the kitchen gives you space to hang pots and utensils. Kitchen supply shops also sell wall- or ceiling-mounted pot holders. This way you use up your air space rights. You can buy space saving shelves, bins, turntables and drawers for kitchen overhead and under-the-counter cabinets. They are available at hardware, department, and houseware stores.

You can hang a tier of narrow shelves on the inside of closet doors. It can hold small items, like extra medical supplies.

A strip of wood studded with cup hooks becomes a belt rack in the clothes closet, a cleaning equipment rack in the broom closet, or a hanging rack for utensils in the kitchen.

Plastic stacking cubes, some of which come outfitted with drawers, can be shoved into a closet for linens, clothing, anything you want. Use stacked vegetable bins for the same purpose.

Of course, you can solve the whole storage problem by owning less.

You Can Always Sublet

Some men may recoil at finding and furnishing an apartment. There *is* an alternative to the park bench. Sublet.

You can sublet both furnished and unfurnished apartments. Be prepared for a wide latitude of interpretation of what people mean by "furnished." It may be furniture that the garbage collector *gave back.* It may be just a few pieces of Early American toss-out. Sometimes the "furniture" looks more like assembled lumber.

Sublet leases usually run for shorter periods of time than the leases on regular rented apartments. Some span only a few months. This can be an advantage. You might want to try out a neighborhood first. You may be taking a job in a town for only a few months and may not be sure if you will be staying longer. You may have just broken up with your wife and want some time to collect your thoughts before you decide on a permanent move.

A furnished sublet obviously costs more than an unfurnished one. But it does give you instant house. Look at it as a dry run for single living.

In a sublet you'll probably have to supply your own linens and some kitchen equipment. Financially, this arrangement may be to your advantage. True, you're paying a higher rent, but you don't have to lay out a large sum for furniture and other space-fillers needed in an empty apartment.

3

Tooling Up the Kitchen

If you're like most men, you find that the kitchen has all the familiarity of a neighborhood in Antarctica. The only reason you know which appliance is the refrigerator is because that's where you keep the beer and ice.

Well, there is no mystery to a kitchen. It's the most functional room in the apartment. Each piece of equipment is there for a purpose. You boil, fry, bake, roast, and just plain heat with the stove. You wash and rinse with the sink. And the refrigerator is for cold storage. Simple.

Any man can learn to manage well in a kitchen. Just arm yourself with a good cookbook, a small assortment of pots and pans, some miscellaneous equipment, and you're ready to attack. You don't have to model your kitchen after Maxim's of Paris. All you need is a simple workshop where you can turn out easy meals for yourself and occasional guests.

The size of your kitchen bears no relationship to function. One friend of mine turns out fabulous dinners from a small cooking area with minimal equipment. The sink is just about large enough for rinsing out a paper cup. The refrigerator is tucked under the counter top, a space large enough for slicing mushrooms, one at a time. Two hot plates provide all the cooking surface. An electric broiler with a glass door provides the "oven." The one item in plentiful supply is ingenuity, and the meals are super.

The Cookbook

Just about the best basic cookbook around is *The Joy of Cooking* by Rombauer and Becker. Almost every bookshop carries it. This one book covers practically everything the neophyte has to know. It'll carry you from hamburgers to crème brulée.

Instructions are clearly stated, easy to follow. You are patiently guided through every recipe. Look, anybody who can read can cook. The book even includes helpful chapters on measuring, ingredients, and other information you should know before you crack your first egg.

There are many other good cookbooks, and they aren't nearly as complicated as you might fear. *Mastering the Art of French Cooking,* Volume One, by Child, Bertholle, and Beck is not nearly as forbidding as it seems. The book contains many recipes for main dishes that take no more than ten minutes to prepare. And they are clearly and simply explained. *The James Beard Cookbook* is another excellent volume. So is Craig Claiborne's *The New York Times Cookbook.* Jean Hewitt's *The New York Times Large Type Cookbook* is exactly what it says: large, easy-to-read type with every recipe on one page or facing pages. But, if you're going to start with just one book, stick to *The Joy of Cooking.*

Pots and Pans

First I want to talk to you about the various materials cookware is made of. Avoid lightweight aluminum. It heats too quickly, scorches food, dents, stains and is a pain to clean. But it's usually cheap. Copper is terrific, but it's expensive. Besides, while it may look great hanging in the kitchen, who's going to keep it polished? Not you.

You have a choice of many excellent materials. Heatproof glass gives you low price, easy cleaning, plus you can see what's happening in the pot. But it is breakable. So, if you're normally *klutzy* and tend to break things, pass on to the next suggestion.

Enamel-coated iron is great. You can cook in it, bring it directly to the table for serving, and clean it easily. But it does chip.

Heavy cast aluminum and stainless are both excellent. They wear well, cook well, and clean well. Teflon-lined pots and pans prevent sticking and let you fry without using grease. You need a special plastic spatula for lifting out eggs so you don't scratch the Teflon surface. Also, they're cleaned with a plastic brush.

As a general rule, remember that heavy pots and pans heat evenly and take high heat without scorching food.

A word of caution. When you first begin buying cookware, don't get carried away. Just buy the basics. You can always add as your repertoire of recipes expands. But, always buy the best quality you can afford. It'll give you better service and it will last longer.

Now for the specific items you need. I've divided them into two categories: essential, those things you should buy immediately, and optional, those items you can buy later as you feel the need for them.

ESSENTIAL

Coffee pot Buy one that makes 6 to 8 cups. Drip pots make the best coffee, but if you prefer a percolator, buy it. There are drip pots using paper filters which make very good coffee.

1 6–7-inch frying pan For scrambling a couple of eggs for yourself or for frying small amounts of food.

1 1½-quart saucepan with cover Buy a fairly squat one so you can cook a package of frozen vegetables in it.

1 3- or 3½-quart saucepan with cover

1 large kettle—8 to 12 quarts For boiling spaghetti, lobster, or chicken. Pick one made of stainless steel. Buy the largest you can store. Be sure it has two handles. They're heavy when full.

1 roasting pan with rack Buy the largest size that will fit into your oven.

2 casseroles with covers—1 quart and 3 quarts Enamelware has the advantage of allowing you to use it directly on flame as well as in the oven. Casseroles can be used for both cooking and serving direct from stove to table.

1 tea kettle It's not strictly for tea; it's for boiling water for any purpose.

OPTIONAL

Coffee pot 2-cup capacity. Makes enough coffee for yourself. Saves washing out a big pot.

1 9–11-inch frying pan with tight fitting cover For frying or sautéing larger amounts of food.

1 10-inch omelet pan Reserve it only for omelets. Never wash it. Just wipe clean after each use with coarse salt and paper towels.

1 griddle

1 5-quart saucepan with cover

1 smaller saucepan (approximately 1 to 2 cups) For melting butter or heating small amounts of liquid, such as Grand Marnier to pour over fresh strawberries.

1 double boiler—1½ quarts The bottom holds hot water; the top, food that can't be safely cooked on direct heat. Also good for reheating food.

1 Dutch Oven—4 to 6 quarts For stews and pot roast.

1 rack for large kettle For steaming fish or clams.

1 baking sheet You may never bake, but this will come in handy for warming store-bought hors d'oeuvres and rolls, or for catching spillovers from casseroles.

1 9-inch pie tin   Serves much the same purpose as the baking sheet but on a smaller scale. And you may want to bake a pie.

Preparation and Measuring Accessories

ESSENTIAL

1 set standard dry measuring cups
1 1-quart heatproof glass measuring cup   With graduated scale on side; a 2-cup size will also do.
1 set standard measuring spoons
1 bottle opener   A beer can opener is perfect.
1 corkscrew   The simple, inexpensive *tire-bouchon* used in French restaurants gives you the best leverage.
1 can opener   The electric models are convenient but expensive. If you buy a wall-mounted can opener, hang it over the sink. If any liquid spills, it will spill into the sink.
1 colander   A footed perforated bowl that is used for draining foods. Buy one at least 10 inches across.
2 sieves (wire mesh strainers)   One small one with very fine mesh; one large one with medium mesh.
1 cutting board   Preferably block maple. Get the largest size you can manage in your kitchen. It's an excellent work surface.
1 juice extractor   Electric models are easier but warrant the expense only if you plan to make yourself fresh orange juice frequently; otherwise, the plain ridged glass cone works fine.
1 wire salad basket   For washing greens and shaking off excess water; also can be used for washing fruits and vegetables.
1 timer   Up to 60-minute capacity. Takes the pressure off keeping track of cooking time while you're busy with something else.
1 salt shaker   For kitchen use only.
1 pepper mill   For kitchen use only.
2 rubber scrapers   One narrow, one wide.
1 meat thermometer   Eliminates guesswork on when the meat is

rare, medium rare, well done, or did you forget to turn on the oven.

1 long-handled, slotted metal spoon   It allows liquid to drain through when you remove food from either gravy or boiling water.

1 long-handled, two-tined fork   Best for spearing a roast.

2 wooden spoons   A couple of different sizes for mixing and stirring.

2 wooden spatulas

1 medium-size wire whisk   You can add other sizes if you find the need for them.

1 medium-size tongs   For retrieving corn and packets from boiling water. For turning meat in broiler or frying pan.

2 metal spatulas   One broad, square-end for flipping hamburgers or pancakes; one perforated skimmer type for draining poached eggs or retrieving vegetables from boiling water.

1 pastry brush   For basting, for coating food with butter, etc.

1 set of 4 mixing bowls   Four sizes, beginning with a 2-cup size; glass or pottery is best.

Scoops   Can be kept in storage jars with flour and sugar.

Vegetable brush   For scrubbing vegetables clean.

OPTIONAL

1 jar wrench   For loosening stubborn jar lids.

1 small funnel   For pouring into jars; used with sieve if you have to strain liquid as you pour.

1 food mill or ricer   For mashed potatoes, apple sauce, or pureeing anything cooked.

1 metal tea infuser   If you're a tea drinker and want a pot of tea with dinner. If you're a purist who shuns tea bags, buy a perforated covered spoon that makes one cup of bulk tea.

1 garlic press   It's easier than mincing.

1 cheese grater   Can be used for nuts also.

1 mortar and pestle   For crushing herbs, garlic, seeds.

2 stainless steel table forks—For beating eggs, stirring, lifting.

1 *rotary egg beater* Heavier ones are easier to work with; electric hand models are easiest but more expensive.

1 *spaghetti lifter* Not essential but a nice convenience for very little money.

1 *bulb baster* For basting roasts.

1 *soup ladle*

1 *box of uncolored toothpicks* Can be used as skewers.

Glass custard cups Handy for holding small amounts of ingredients while you're cooking. Also can be used for puddings.

1 *splatter shield* Fits over frying pan and prevents grease from splattering over stove; saves time cleaning up.

Cutting and Peeling

ESSENTIAL

1 *vegetable peeler* Also good for sharpening pencils.

1 *kitchen shears* Medium length blades, for mincing, etc.

1 *sharpening steel* Easiest and best way to keep your knives keen.

2 *paring knives* One 2-inch blade; one 4-inch blade. (A note about knives: carbon steel blades are best; they give you the sharpest cutting edge, but they require more care since they rust if left wet.)

1 *bread knife with serrated edge*

1 *slicing knife* 8- to 9-inch blade.

1 *chef's knife* 7 to 9-inch blade. Buy a good heavy one because you'll give this a lot of use for slicing, chopping, and mincing.

OPTIONAL

1 *grapefruit knife* Unless you don't eat grapefruit.

1 *frozen food knife* You may want to use only half a package of

frozen vegetables and then save the rest for a subsequent dinner.

1 *poultry shears*

1 *magnetic knife rack*   Wall mounted; keeps most frequently used knives handy.

Cleaning Up the Mess

Sponges   Cellulose, available in packages at supermarkets; pick a size comfortable to your hand.

Dish towels   At least 6 so you don't run out of clean ones.

Plastic scouring pad   For scouring enamelware and Teflon.

Stainless scouring pad   Tougher; good for metal pots and pans, but will mark enamelware.

Dish drainer pad and rack   Not necessary if you're lucky enough to have a dishwasher.

Dish pan   Forget it if you have a dishwasher.

Garbage pail with cover

Garbage bags

Soap

Detergent   Dishwashing liquids if you have to wash by hand; a special dishwasher detergent if you have a machine.

Keeping the Heat Off

Pot holders   Buy at least two. If you have metal kitchen cabinets, buy pot holders with magnets sewn into the edge. You can hang them on doors or on the stove.

Asbestos mat   To put under casseroles or whenever you want to keep the heat very low.

Fire extinguisher   Keep a small foam-type handy for fat fires.

Electrical Equipment

There are all kinds of electrical cooking gadgets and accessories. Some make a lot of sense; some are only current fad waves and end up collecting dust in the closet. Besides, if you're watching your money, don't squander it on expensive electrical gadgetry. Buy only what you need. You can indulge your idiosyncracies later on. Here are a few electrical appliances that are good to start with.

2-slice toaster
Broiler   Easier to clean than an oven and it won't heat up the kitchen as much.
Hot plate   Optional, but it does keep the coffee hot at the table.
Juicer   Only if you squeeze fresh juice a lot.
Hand mixer   Not necessary, but convenient if you do a lot of cooking.
Blender   Also a luxury, but helpful for mixing certain drinks as well as for easy mixing, stirring, pureeing or other fine chopping.

Storage

Wine rack   12-bottle capacity.
Refrigerator dishes with covers   Several manufacturers make excellent assortments, ranging from small sizes of less than a cup capacity to big sizes for storing bread or large amounts of cooked foods, such as stews.
Canisters   Modern versions of old-fashioned apothecary jars are available in assorted sizes and provide excellent air-tight storage for flour, sugar, or anything else that needs this type of care.
Bin for potatoes and onions   You can also store these vegetables in baskets.

Juice jar
Jars   Assorted sizes with screw tops; save the ones that peanut butter, jams or herrings come in.
Waxed paper, aluminum foil, plastic wrap, plastic bags
3-way or 4-way paper dispenser   Holds paper toweling, aluminum foil, plastic wrap, and waxed paper.

Serving and Eating

Acquiring serving and eating tools can become an endless process. Listed below is a basic inventory which will get you through most any meal. As you go along, you may find the need for additional pieces, such as more glasses or a couple of small serving bowls or platters. Buy as you need.

Dishes   Buy a basic set of service for at least 4 people; 6 is better if you can afford it. Include a covered vegetable dish and an open one. If you're a big tea drinker, buy a tea pot.
Silverware   Here, too, buy a basic service for 4 or 6, but add extra teaspoons. In addition, you'll need some serving pieces: serving spoon, serving fork, salad spoon and fork, cake server.
Glassware   Water tumblers, juice glasses, wine glasses (pick a wine glass with a large bowl). A couple of shot glasses.
Salad bowl   Can be wood or glass or can match your china.
Serving platters   At least one large size plus two or three assorted smaller sizes.
Carving board   Oak with a well and drains carved in it.
Place mats   A couple of sets with matching napkins for company; cork or woven plastic that can be wiped clean for daily use.
Napkins   Paper or cloth.
Cork trivets   Three assorted sizes to put under hot dishes for protection of table top.
Trays   One large size, one smaller; saves a lot of walking back and forth from kitchen to table.

Salt shaker and pepper mill   Yes, you can use a pepper shaker with commercially ground pepper. But fresh ground pepper is infinitely better.

Bread baskets   A long one for French bread, a round or oval one for other breads or rolls. A couple of small ones for crackers when you serve cheese or spreads with drinks.

Ice bucket

A jigger for measuring when mixing drinks

Water pitcher   Big enough for mixing drinks.

Carving tools   You can use your kitchen knives.

You Don't Need It But Why Not Have It

An earthenware crock which you keep out on a counter to hold utensils you use frequently: wooden spoons, measuring spoons, cheese slicer, whisks, etc.

Tiny 1-inch magnets which you can use to post notes to yourself on the cabinet doors (if the doors are metal) or to hold a recipe at eye level while you're cooking or a shopping list to which you add as you need.

Save a plastic bleach bottle. Trim off the top, leaving a two or three inch rim. Good to use in the sink as a receptacle for garbage while you're cleaning vegetables or doing other food preparations. Punch holes in the bottom to allow water to drain out.

Paper cup dispenser. Saves washing glasses.

Bulletin board. A handy place to post notes to yourself, newspaper clippings, theatre tickets, shopping lists, laundry receipts, etc.

Paper napkin holder. Attach it to the wall; keeps them handy.

Towel ring for dish towels. Otherwise, what do you do with them?

Kitchen clock or clock radio.

If you're short on money, you don't have to—you can't—buy all your kitchen equipment at once. Start with the basics: coffee pot, skillet, a couple of saucepans. Buy china, silver, and glassware that's open stock (meaning it's always available for purchase in the future). Start with service for two and add pieces as you can afford or need them.

Any of your women friends, sisters, sisters-in-law, mother, or, possibly, your ex-wife will be glad to guide you on essentials. Sometimes salespeople may be helpful. Don't let some housewares "expert" overwhelm you with an inexhaustible list of "essentials." If you find that you overcooked the roast, make a note to pick up a meat thermometer so you don't repeat the mistake.

When John was divorced, money wasn't a problem. Once he found an apartment, he practically duplicated his wife's kitchen equipment. Unfortunately, he didn't duplicate her interest in cooking. True, he cooks for himself, but he mainly broils steaks or fish or does simple sautéing. There's nothing wrong with this. It's just that owning a soufflé dish doesn't improve the taste of a frozen TV dinner.

Elliott, on the other hand, really got into the cooking scene. One reason was that his three children visited him every weekend. He turned making dinner into a family activity that the kids enjoyed. It also nourished his own interest in cooking. As his skill increased, he found himself browsing in hotel and restaurant supply stores the way he used to forage in hardware stores. He learned about specialized cooking equipment. He now knows that a Charlotte mold has nothing to do with 36-26-36.

Once you own the basic equipment, match your acquisitions to your needs and your pocketbook.

4

How to Buy and Store
Peanut Butter
and Other Foods You Eat

If you were married, you probably did some marketing for your wife. This at least gave you some clues about that modern maze of efficiency called a supermarket. But that list you clutched in your hand represented the needs for a whole family. It's a totally different ball game when you shop for yourself.

Your wife or mother bought in quantities that would be excessive for you. She bought "economy" sizes. She bought multiples of many items. Her repertoire of recipes was much greater than yours currently is, so she stocked many items you won't use.

When Don's wife walked out on him, she left the kitchen intact. The cupboards were stocked with unfamiliar items. After six months, he cleaned house and got rid of every food item he had not used during that period. He has yet to replace one item he discarded.

It's obvious that if you're one person, you buy in small quantities.

You buy the smaller sizes. However, if you've got a favorite food that you use up with astonishing rapidity, buy accordingly. If you can't keep your finger out of the peanut butter jar, buy the larger size. After a few jars of peanut butter you can buy larger size clothes too.

As a single man you will probably tend to eat more meals out than you did before. Dating plus dinner invitations will frequently keep you out of the kitchen. Therefore you should buy perishables only as you need them. This includes fresh fruits and vegetables which are best if bought just when you are ready to use them. The fresher the better.

I'm not recommending daily trips to the market. But remember that your schedule is more flexible now. You can decide Tuesday afternoon not to eat home Tuesday night. So once-a-week shopping for perishables can mean a lot of wilted lettuce in the refrigerator. You can always stock emergency supplies in the freezer compartment of your refrigerator. If you decide at the last minute, after the stores are closed, that you will eat home Tuesday night, you can. But I'm not suggesting you keep lettuce in the freezer.

Once you've set up your basic food supply, it's a simple matter of replacing or buying as you need. It's a good idea to make a shopping list. Men are normally more impulsive buyers of food than women. It's okay to be reckless about chocolate-covered grasshoppers, but at least have a reminder that you're down to your last roll of paper towels. Supermarkets are constantly stocking new convenience items to accommodate the working man or woman: canned or frozen sauces, new frozen main dishes. Be on the lookout for new you-don't-have-to-cook-dinner products.

There are certain staples you should keep on hand. Ignore any which you know you will never eat.

Sugar

Salt (regular table salt; coarse Kosher salt for cooking)

Flour (buy in 2 lb. bags. You'll use it up slowly)

Olive oil

Mayonnaise

Hot cereals (There are "instant" products available which give you the flavor if not the texture of more slowly cooked cereals)

Rice (there are packaged pre-cooked rice products which can be prepared in minutes)

Spices (start with peppercorns, basil, tarragon, thyme, chives, parsley, dry mustard, bay leaf. You can always add others if you need them)

Vegetable oil or peanut oil

Wine vinegar

Chili sauce

Catsup

Mustard

Coffee (instant or ground. Ground is better; instant is a hot beverage)

Tea (bags or, for heavy tea drinkers, bulk)

Dry cereals

Spaghetti or linguini (The dry packaged type, not the canned)

Salted or unsalted crackers (Unsalted is better with cheese)

Cookies

Peanut butter

Worcestershire sauce or steak sauce

Assorted jams, jellies, and marmalade

Salad dressing (These are also available in a dry form to which you add water, vinegar, and oil)

Jello and puddings (Here, too, you can buy "instant" mixes)

Keep on hand these foods which come in cans or jars. Buy small sizes. You can buy a couple of larger sizes for last minute company or when the kids visit.

Soups (There are also dry-mix soups available)

Vegetables (You may prefer fresh or frozen varieties)

Juices

Fruits (for easy desserts)

Spaghetti sauce

Clam sauce

Tuna fish, salmon, and sardines

Tomato sauce and tomato paste

Beef stew, chicken stew, chow mein (You try them and let me know how they are)

Olives (green and black)

Pickles

Beverages to keep on hand:

Beer and hard liquor, by choice

Club soda

Quinine water

Cola drinks

Ginger ale

If you have a freezer, you can stock some things for future use. Be sure any frozen foods you buy are firmly frozen, wrappings undamaged, at the time of purchase.

Vegetables

Fruits

Juices (Fresh-squeezed orange juice soon will be as rare as the buggy whip)

Main dishes (The best aren't bad and, if you feel lazy, it's dinner-without-cooking)

Bread (sliced, so you can defrost only what you need)

Rolls and croissants

Cake and pie

Ice cream (Particularly ice cream pops, for children)

Whether or not you keep cocktail snacks around is a matter of personal choice. These don't obligate you to give a party, but you may like them just for yourself or for when you have someone up for a drink. Supermarkets usually have a whole section devoted to these waistline expanders. A few you might pick up are:

Peanuts

Potato chips

Pretzels

Small whole salami

Canned paté

Flavored crackers (garlic-

flavored, cheese-flavored, etc.)

Frozen, jarred or spray-canned dips

Cocktail tidbits such as caponata

With the exception of hard cheeses, which can be stored over a period of time, dairy products should be bought only as needed. If you buy a large chunk of cheese, cut off what you need and leave the remainder in the refrigerator. Cheese dries out prematurely if constantly taken in and out of cold storage.

Milk (Unless you drink a lot of it, buy pint containers)

Eggs (Buy a half-dozen at a time, so you don't have them

around a long time getting stale)

Butter, sweet or salted (Keep a small amount handy; keep a reserve in the freezer.)

Produce also should be bought as close to actual time of use as possible. Buy enough for two or three days at most. There are a few items you should keep on hand:

Garlic

Lemons (or lemon or lime juice)

Potatoes (about 1 lb., medium size)

Onions (about 1 lb., medium size)

Meat, too, is bought as needed. For boneless meat, figure about a half-pound per serving. Some things keep a few days, so you can buy a couple of items in advance and save yourself daily trips to the butcher or meat counter of your supermarket. Wrap loosely in wax paper and store near the freezer compartment. If it comes in plastic wrapping, remove wrapping unless you plan to use it immediately. Do not wash meat. Just wipe clean with a damp cloth. Air circulation helps protect meat's quality. You can also keep a supply of steaks and chops in the freezer.

One of the great conveniences that has sprung up in recent years is stores that sell foods already cooked and ready for the table. The larger the city you live in, the more choice you'll have. These foods generally need no more than a short time for heating before being ready to eat. Some, obviously, can be eaten cold. Among the types of stores that you will learn to love as man's best friend are:

Delicatessens   Jewish, Italian, Scandinavian, and German. Each features ethnic dishes which prove that what's important is not where your family came from but how long do you have to heat their cooking.

Chicken stores   Here you can purchase rotisserie-cooked pieces or whole chickens.

Chinese restaurants   Many feature take-out service.

Supermarkets   Many have delicatessen counters that feature ready-cooked foods.

Bakeries   Particularly good are French bakeries which sometimes have frozen *quiches Lorraine* or other specialties.

Catering establishments   Some prepare their specialties in individual portions for retail trade.

Pizza parlors   Some carry additional items, such as spaghetti sauce.

Storing Foods

Many of the packaged and wrapped foods you buy will carry storage directions on the package. They may advise you to keep something in a cool, dry place, refrigerated, out of the sun, away from the heat and other similar cautions. Items that require storage away from the heat should not be kept in cupboards over the stove. These tend to get warmer because of cooking heat.

Here are a few general rules to keep in mind about storing foods:

1. Dry foods, such as flour, cereals, crackers, unopened jams, sugar store well at room temperature.
2. Spices store at room temperature, but keep away from heat to prevent deterioration of flavor.
3. Breadstuffs that will be used within a few days keep best refrigerated.
4. Open syrups, jams, honey should be refrigerated. If they granulate, place jar in a pan of warm water until contents of jar reliquefy.
5. Open jars of mayonnaise, salad dressing, peanut butter, and other foods with high fat content keep best refrigerated.
6. Store eggs in the refrigerator covered or in original carton. Since shells are porous, they lose flavor and moisture if not covered.
7. Keep hard cheeses, butter, and margarine tightly wrapped or in a covered container to preserve flavor and prevent loss of moisture.
8. Open cooking and salad oils should be refrigerated. If they solidify or become cloudy, don't worry. It doesn't affect the flavor. They liquefy again at room temperature or when heated.

9. Fruits should be kept refrigerated after they ripen. Store bananas at room temperature. Store unripened fruit and vegetables at room temperature. Setting them in the sun will hasten ripening.
10. Keep potatoes, lemons, and onions in a cool, dry, well-ventilated place.
11. Fruits and berries keep best if left unwashed until ready to be eaten.
12. Most vegetables keep better in the refrigerator.
13. Salad greens and green leafy vegetables should be washed, dried with paper towels, and then stored in a "crispers" or in plastic bags in refrigerator.
14. Meat, poultry, and fish store best when loosely wrapped before placing in the refrigerator. Tight wrapping encourages spoilage.
15. Spaghetti and noodles, once packages are opened, should be stored in jars, plastic bags, or other tightly sealed containers. Unprotected, they attract homeless, hungry bugs.
16. As a general rule, air in a refrigerator is coldest nearest the freezer. Keep meat, poultry, fish, dairy products, eggs near top; fruits and vegetables, near bottom. In newer models with a separate freezer, temperature is usually uniform throughout the refrigerator compartment.
17. If you are storing open cans or jars in the refrigerator, cover them. Much better is to transfer to a jar with a lid.
18. Unused onion can be stored in a sealed jar or in tightly wrapped plastic in the refrigerator. Cut lemon and lime also last longer if wrapped.
19. Parsley keeps much longer if, after washing and drying, it is stood up in a jar filled with enough water to immerse stems but not leaves. Cover jar.
20. To have a supply of ice cubes always handy, empty ice cube trays into drip tray under freezer. If you have a separate freezer, empty trays into plastic bags and store immediately, while cubes are still dry and have not started to melt, so they won't stick together.

21. When arranging groceries in overhead cabinets, first line shelves with foil, shelf paper, or rubber shelf liner. Then store in order of frequency of use from the bottom up.
22. Opened cans of coffee retain freshness longer if refrigerated.

5

Adam in the Kitchen Without Eve: Thirty Simple One-Man Meals

As a single man you will be eating a lot of your meals out. First, because there are fewer single men than single women, you are a favorable statistic. This will earn you a lot of dinner invitations. Second, you will be taking dates out to dinner. But, eventually you will have to take that cooking equipment you bought and get it together with that food you stocked in the kitchen.

Restrict yourself to simple dinners. You probably will be cooking after a day of work when your energy is at a low ebb. Also, you probably have little cooking experience, so everything will seem difficult at first. Don't make it more so by trying to handle a Beef Wellington the first time you sail into the kitchen. Simple dinners made at home can be delicious, healthful, ego-gratifying and a damned sight more enjoyable than dinner alone in a restaurant.

In the beginning you can rely heavily on ready-cooked and frozen foods mentioned in an earlier chapter. This will at least familiarize you with the logistics of assembling a meal and heating up the various elements of your dinner. Meanwhile, leaf through your cookbook and seek out things that seem obviously easy to make. In any basic cookbook there are dozens of them.

Get into the habit of setting the table for yourself. It takes only a minute and makes the meal more pleasant. Eating over the kitchen sink is fine if you're a heavy drooler, but in that case you might find the bathtub more satisfactory.

In the meals I suggest later on in this chapter, I eliminate a first course or appetizer. If you wish, you can always start off with juice (from a can), soup (from a can), or herring in cream sauce, pickling brine, or wine sauce. I assume that while you are preparing dinner, you have armed yourself with a drink. Or perhaps you have wisely taken some time to relax when you arrive home. While enjoying your drink, you can open a jar of herring, some cheese or peanut butter, apply same to crackers and—presto—instant appetizer.

Many frozen vegetables, fruits, and soups are packaged so as to make two-to-three portions. Frozen food packages can be cut in half before thawing. Rewrap the unused portion to protect the exposed cut surface and return to the freezer for future use. Be sure you retain the cooking instructions printed on the label. Soups, of course, you must make all at once. The leftovers can be stored in the refrigerator for another meal.

During the week rely on broiled or sautéed main dishes. They are quickest to cook. After a day's work, you don't want to get involved in an hour or more of food preparation. On weekends you can spread out to more ambitious enterprises like roasts or stews. Roasts or stews more than pay for themselves in time because they last through more than one meal. Use some during the week when time is more precious; freeze some for some future meals.

In any meal where I suggest two vegetables and a salad you may want to eliminate one of them. If you're avoiding potatoes, substitute another vegetable or make a bigger salad. Fresh vegetables in season are always preferable to frozen ones. But, if you prefer frozen ones because of their convenience, use them.

Vegetables are best when cooked in the French method, which

means immersion in a pot of boiling water, cooking time counted from the time the water returns to a boil. Add salt at the same time you add the vegetable. It sets the color. Naturally, cooking time varies with the vegetable. Some cook in only minutes; others take longer. Vegetables should retain a crunchiness when cooked. Unfortunately, many of us were raised in homes where vegetables had texture, flavor, and nutrition cooked right out of them.

With meats, cooking time is determined by whether you like your meat rare, medium rare or well done. Pork is always cooked well done. When you buy meat, ask the butcher for suggested cooking time. Same thing with the fish market. Always get the trimmed cooking weight of anything you buy. Meat prewrapped in supermarkets usually carries the weight on the price ticket.

If you are thawing meat stored in your freezer, take it out in the morning before you go to work. Wrap it in several layers of newspaper. This will allow it to thaw while remaining chilled. It will also prevent the loss of juices, which, if allowed to run off, means a dry piece of meat.

One caution. Many times you may be cooking with a lot of fat. If the fat catches fire, first turn off the burner or oven. If possible, retrieve your dinner with tongs or a long-handled fork. If you have no fire extinguisher, smother the fire with baking soda or salt. If you're cooking in a skillet, simply cover the skillet with its lid to cut off the oxygen supply.

If you have fat left over after cooking, don't pour it down the sink drain. It can cause clogging. Save an empty can, pour the fat in this and store it in the refrigerator. When the can is full, toss it out and start over again with another empty can.

Where a recipe calls for frying or sautéing in butter, you can prevent butter from burning and the food from sticking to the pan surface by adding a few drops of vegetable oil to the butter. You add the oil first and let it thinly coat the bottom of the pan.

If you like poached eggs for breakfast, you can make a cooking ring in which to poach them by merely removing the top and bottom of a tuna fish can.

If you want to bake a potato but it's too hot to turn on the oven, you have an alternative. Cook it in a can large enough to hold it, such as an empty coffee can, first placing in the can a raised platform for the potato. This can be done with an old jar lid or crushed aluminum foil. Pierce the potato to allow steam to escape (otherwise the potato will burst), cover the can, place on a burner on top of the stove with the lowest heat possible. In about 20 minutes the potato is done.

Wherever a recipe calls for brushing ingredients with butter, oil, or some other fat and you're trying to cut down on calories, squeeze a lemon over the food instead. Just be sure you use enough juice to prevent drying out. Squeeze the lemon through cheesecloth or nylon netting to prevent it from splattering. Cut lemon, incidentally, stores better under refrigeration if wrapped in plastic.

If you're a bread eater, you can buy a great variety of frozen breads, rolls, biscuits and croissants at the supermarket. Unused fresh bread can be frozen. Desserts are no problem. Fruit with cheese is obviously simple. So are ice cream, cookies, or bakery items. Here too, if you shop the frozen food cabinets, you may save time but lose your waistline. Besides frozen fruits, which often tend to be sweet and syrupy, you can buy tarts, pies and cakes. Some merely have to be thawed (though they are always nicer warm); others require a short baking time.

Now we're ready to eat!

In cooking, as in other important pleasurable activities, timing is essential. How do you make everything come out together at the same time?

With your first meals, get most preparations out of the way before you start cooking a single thing. Set the table. Prepare the salad (without the dressing), cover and store in the refrigerator. Wash the vegetables and do any slicing and cutting that may be necessary. If meat or fish has to be breaded or rolled in flour, do it in advance. Assemble all the ingredients you need so that they're immediately available the instant you need them.

While waiting for the steak to finish, sit back and fantasize winning that last argument with your wife or doing more pushups than your teenage son. Or you can plan a seductive dinner for two which you will climax with a soufflé full of aphrodisiacs concocted from your own secret formula.

With experience, you will learn to dovetail cooking times for various foods. Then you will be able to handle part of the preparations while other things are cooking.

Before you do any cooking, read the recipe carefully. Look for instructions for cooling ingredients, getting them down to room temperature or pre-warming, or soaking a length of time before use. Get in the habit of wearing an apron. Grease splatters; certain fruits and vegetables stain permanently. All sorts of mishaps occur. You can buy very handsome chef's or butcher's aprons or even a machinist's apron.

You may have absolutely no interest in cooking but don't want to eat out. You could go through your whole life living off of frozen and prepared foods. A casual study of any supermarket's frozen food section reveals an ever increasing number of items ranging from cocktail hors d'oeuvres to desserts. They all achieve their main purpose which is to provide nutrition without effort. And if an idea achieves its main objective without effort, I suppose this has merit. If you subscribe to this philosophy, you'll love artificial insemination.

To give you an idea of the variety available to you, here is a list of frozen foods found in just one large supermarket. I've divided it into categories. If you decide that this is the route you prefer, just proceed on to the frozen wasteland. Be prepared for the fact that frozen foods are more expensive than freshly prepared foods. If you prefer to have greater control over what goes into your stomach and are just a bit more ambitious, proceed on to the simple dinners I suggest.

The frozen foods listed below are ready to eat after following extremely simple instructions. Some you merely pop into a toaster; others are dropped into boiling water. A few require a heated oven. You may have to add water or milk. This should make the level of required skill clear.

Breakfast

Juices
Waffles
Pancake batter
French toast
Pancakes
Donuts
Omelets

Corn muffins
Blueberry muffins
Apple Danish
Pecan Danish
Croissants
Coffee rings

(Complete prepared breakfasts are also available, featuring pancakes and sausage or omelets and bacon.)

Lunch

Soups
Cheese blintzes
Potato blintzes
Blueberry blintzes
Potato pancakes

Macaroni and cheese
Cheese soufflé
Corn soufflé
Welsh rarebit

(Check the dinner selections for anything in the main course or dessert items that you would want to use for lunch.)

Cocktail Hour

Clams Casino
Chopped chicken livers
Cheese appetizers

Cheese puffs
Frankfurters in puff paste
Assorted hors d'oeuvres

Dinner

APPETIZERS
Soups
Crab meat cocktail
Butterfly shrimp

Shrimp with cocktail sauce
Clam cocktail with sauce

MAIN COURSES

Fish and Shellfish

Fried shrimp
Shrimp scampi
Shore dinner
Breaded fish fillets

Fish sticks
Tuna noodle casserole
Fish 'n chips
Lobster Newburg

Chicken or Turkey

Chicken with noodles
Chicken in a basket
Fried chicken
Turkey pie
Chicken pie
Creamed chicken
Chicken croquette

Chicken Divan
Baked chicken breasts with
  gravy
Chicken with dumplings in
  cheese sauce
Turkey Tetrazzini

Beef, Pork and Veal

Roast beef hash
Salisbury steak
Beef kabobs
Corned beef hash
Beef and noodles
Stuffed green peppers
Stuffed cabbage
Beef and macaroni

Ham, cheese and macaroni
Beef burgundy
Beef Stroganoff
Beef and peppers
Beef stew
Beef pie
Swedish meatballs
Breaded veal filled with cheese

Italian Dishes

Lasagna
Pizza
Meat ravioli
Cheese ravioli

Cheese filled manicotti
Baked ziti
Eggplant parmigiana

Chinese Dishes

Fried rice with pork
Meat and shrimp egg roll
Chicken chow mein

Shrimp chow mein
Chinese Vegetables

Complete Dinners (Some include vegetables and dessert).

Chicken dinner
Turkey dinner
Fried chicken dinner
Beef dinner
Swiss steak dinner
Ham dinner

Loin of pork dinner
Veal parmigiana dinner
Spaghetti and meatball dinner
Meat loaf dinner
Mexican dinner

VEGETABLES

Scalloped potatoes
French fried potatoes
Hash brown potatoes
Whipped potatoes
Whole boiled potatoes
Buttered parsley potatoes
Candied sweet potatoes
Corn on the cob
Corn niblets
Corn with peas and tomatoes
Spinach soufflé
Leaf spinach
Creamed spinach
Chopped spinach
Sliced carrots

Green beans with mushrooms
Italian green beans
Baby lima beans
Broccoli spears
Broccoli spears in hollandaise
  sauce
Chopped broccoli au gratin
Asparagus spears
Asparagus in hollandaise sauce
Brussel sprouts
Brussel sprouts and cheese
  casserole
Zucchini
Mashed turnips
Breaded eggplant slices

Carrot nuggets
Carrots and peas
Escalloped apples
Cauliflower
Cauliflower au gratin
Cauliflower and sour cream
  casserole
Rice pilaf
Spanish rice
Green beans
Green beans French style
Green beans with toasted
  almonds

Onion rings
Creamed onions
Whole mushrooms
Okra
Summer squash
Artichoke hearts
Peas
Peas and celery
Sliced beets with orange glaze
Mixed vegetables (plain, French,
  Italian, Danish, Mexican,
  Japanese, Bavarian or
  Chinese style)

DESSERTS
Whipped cream substitutes to
  use where desired
Pineapple chunks
Strawberries
Blueberries
Cupcakes
Almond fudge cake
Chocolate chip cake
Chocolate swirl cake
Chocolate cake
Devil's food cake
Raisin cake
Blueberry crumb cake
Crumb cake
Apple pecan cake
Pound cake
Lemon pound cake
Raisin pound cake
Date and nut cake
Apple and walnut cake
Orange curl cake
Cinnamon nut cake

Pecan coffee cake
Blueberry shortcake
Chocolate eclairs
Cream puffs
Turnovers: apple, blueberry or
  raspberry
Pie tarts: apple, blueberry,
  lemon or cherry
Cream cheese cake
Strawberry cheese cake
Deep dish apple pie
Apple pie
Cherry pie
Blueberry pie
Strawberry cream pie
Neapolitan cream pie
Dutch apple crumb pie
Lemon meringue pie
Banana cream pie
Chocolate pudding
Vanilla pudding

There is also an assortment of rolls and breads, including garlic bread.

For those who want to make their own dinners with fresh ingredients, the following charts should be helpful. They are guides for cooking commonly used meats, fish and vegetables. Always start meat or fish at room temperature unless a recipe specifies otherwise. Before broiling, remove the rack from the broiler pan and line the pan with aluminum foil. This catches dripping and makes cleaning up easier. If you prefer, you can buy disposable heavy aluminum broiler pans. Brushing the broiler rack with oil or butter prevents foods from sticking. This is especially important when broiling fish, which breaks easily.

Broiling Timetable

Set oven at Broil. (Pre-heat broiler, broiler pan and rack for 10 minutes, 3 or 4 inches from heat.)

	Thickness	*Approximate minutes per side*		
		Rare	Medium	Well Done
BEEF Hamburger	1 in.	4	6	8
Steak, Club, Porter-	1 in.	5 to 6	7	8 to 9
house, Delmonico, Filet	1½ in.	9	10	12 to 15
Mignon, Rib, T-Bone	2 in.	10 to 12	15 to 18	20 to 22
Steak, Sirloin	1 in.	8 to 9	10	11 to 13
	1½ in.	12	14	17
Flank Steak	1 to 1½ in.	5		
Frankfurters		(Turn occasionally until evenly browned).		
HAM SLICE Ready-to-eat	¾ in.			7 to 9
LAMB Rib or	1 in.	8	10	14 or more
Loin Chops	1½ in.	10	12	16 or more
	2 in.	12	16	20 or more
PORK Chops	1 in.			18 to 23
CHICKEN Quartered				30 on first side;
(Place chicken 6 to 8 in. from heat; brush with melted butter.)				15 to 30 on other
FISH (Brush fish and broiler rack with butter. Place rack 2 in. from heat.)				
Fillets	¼ to 1 in.			5 to 8
Steaks	½ to 1½ in.			6 to 15
Dressed Whole				6 to 8

Vegetable Cooking Timetable

This is for fresh vegetables only; frozen and canned vegetables carry instructions on the package. Substitute for fresh vegetables if fresh aren't available or you really don't want to bother. Wash all fresh vegetables thoroughly before cooking. Bring pot of water to boil. Time cooking from when water returns to boil after vegetables and salt are added. Cook uncovered unless instructed otherwise. Cook until tender. Test tenderness with a fork or knife tip. You can always taste a piece. It should be tender but not mushy.

Vegetable	Preparation	Approximate Cooking Time (Minutes)
Asparagus	Break off woody stems. Remove tough scales.	10 to 20 depending on thickness. Boil slowly.
Beets	Cut off stems, leaving about 1 inch.	Cook covered. 20 to 30. Slip off skins after cooking.
Broccoli	Remove large leaves and ends of stems. Peel and split large stems lengthwise.	Boil slowly. 5 to 7.
Brussel sprouts	Cut off stem ends.	Boil slowly. 10 to 15.
Carrots	Remove ends. Scrub well with brush. Scrape or pare thinly. If thick, cut in half or quarters.	Cook covered in a small amount of water with butter. Whole: 15 to 30. Sliced: 6 to 20.
Cauliflower	Remove outer leaves and stalks. Leave whole or break into flowerlets.	Boil slowly. Whole: 15 to 25. Flowerlets: 8 to 15.

Vegetable	Preparation	Approximate Cooking Time (Minutes)
Corn on the cob	Just before cooking, remove husks and silk.	Boil rapidly. 3 to 5.
Green beans	Remove ends; leave whole or cut on diagonal into 1 or 2 in. pieces.	Boil slowly. 10 to 15.
Peas	Shell just before cooking.	Boil slowly. 4 to 10.
Potatoes	Baked: scrub; rub with butter; puncture with fork.	45 to 60 (oven at 375 degrees).
	Boiled: pare; remove eyes.	Cook covered. Whole: 20 to 40. Cut-up: 10 to 15.
Spinach	Unless pre-washed, wash several times, lifting leaves out of water each time.	Boil slowly. 4 to 6.
Squash		
Summer	Remove tip. Scrub well.	Boil slowly. 15 to 20.
Acorn	Cut in half; remove seeds; grease skin.	Bake at 375 degrees 1 to 1½ hours.
Zucchini	Scrub well; remove stem ends; cut into slices.	Boil slowly. 10 to 20.

Here are some easy dinners you can use for starters. Check charts for cooking time. All are preceded by cocktails for one. If you don't want wine with meal, drink beer. Sweet drinks tend to kill the taste of everything. All vegetables are fresh except where frozen ones are specified.

Where salad is specified, I mean a tossed green salad, not a wedge of iceberg lettuce. Iceberg is all texture and little taste. Try Boston lettuce, leaf lettuce, raw spinach, escarole, chicory, Bibb or mix them all up. Add a little chopped parsley and dill for a more flavorful salad. If you like, you can also slice some scallions or Spanish onions or crumbled cheese into the salad. Your choices are infinite. There's no cooking involved: just tear up some greens. Add dressing just before eating. Where "cake," "pie" or "fruit" is specified for dessert, make your own choice.

Dinner No. 1

Broiled Steak

Baked Potato   Sliced Carrots

Green Salad

Red Wine

Coffee or Tea   Melon or Fruit in Season

You need: A one-inch thick steak, ½ to ¾ lbs.; one Idaho potato; three or four carrots; salad greens; fruit.

Preparation: Prepare salad and store in refrigerator. Get steak to room temperature. Trim off excess fat. Cut carrots into thin slices. Wash and grease potato; puncture with fork. Preheat oven to 375 degrees. Put potato in oven. Since the potato takes 45 to 60 minutes, you will want to put it in well ahead of the steak and carrots. Check the charts for steak and carrots. Simple subtraction gives you approximate lead time for the potato. At proper time, raise oven temperature to "broil" and place steak on broiler. Place carrots in saucepan with a little water; add a pinch of salt; pepper; ⅛ teaspoon of ground ginger; a pat of butter. Simmer gently until tender. Check degree of doneness of steak by making tiny slash in meat.

Dinner No. 2

Pan Broiled Steak

Baked Potato   Broccoli

Sliced Tomato

Red Wine

Coffee or Tea   Cheese and Crackers (Unsalted)

You need: A one-inch shell steak, ½ to ¾ lbs.; bunch of broccoli; (use ⅓ for a serving); one Idaho potato; one tomato; cheeses.

Preparation: Slice tomato or cut into wedges. Leave at room temperature. Remove cheese from refrigerator to allow it to reach room temperature. Trim excess fat off steak. Prepare potato and figure approximate cooking time as in Dinner No. 1. Bring kettle of water to boil for broccoli. Cook as per chart instructions. Serve with lemon wedges. Heat heavy skillet with enough oil and butter combined to coat bottom. When oil and butter are hot but not burning, add steak over moderate heat. Cook about 3 or 4 minutes on each side. Remove steak to hot platter. Pour out all except a tablespoon of drippings from skillet. Add a splash of cognac, dry vermouth or red wine to skillet. Turn up flame. With wooden spoon, scrape bottom of skillet and blend in with liquid. Pour over steak.

Dinner No. 3

Sautéed Soft Shell Crabs
Corn on the Cob   Green Salad
Beer or Chilled White Wine
Coffee or Tea   Ice Cream

You Need: two or three softshell crabs; one or two ears of corn; lemon; salad greens; ice cream.

Preparation: Ask fish market to clean crabs. At home, wash crabs, dry them well with paper towels. Prepare salad and store in refrigerator. Put up water to boil for corn. Add a teaspoon of salt to water. Remove husk and silk from corn. Dredge crabs in flour. Heat 2 tablespoons of butter and a splash of oil in skillet. When butter and oil mixture is hot, place crabs in skillet. Sauté on both sides until brown and crisp. This should take just a few minutes. Season with salt and pepper while cooking. Put on hot plate, pour juices in skillet over crabs. Serve with lemon wedges. Cook corn while eating crabs.

Dinner No. 4

Broiled Frankfurters
Baked Beans   Potato Salad
Cole Slaw or Sauerkraut
Sour Pickles   Beer
Coffee or Tea   Pound Cake

You need: two or three all-beef frankfurters; one small can baked beans; ½ lb. potato salad; ¼ lb. cole slaw or sauerkraut; pound cake.

Preparation: Buy cole slaw, potato salad, and pickles at a delicatessen. Broil frankfurters split or whole until brown on all sides. Put beans in saucepan over low heat. Stir occasionally until heated through.

Dinner No. 5

Sautéed Bay Scallops

Green Beans   Baked Potato

Sliced Tomato and Lettuce Salad

Beer or Chilled White Wine

Coffee   Pie

You need: ¼ to ⅓ lb. bay scallops; lemon, ¼ lb. green beans; one Idaho potato; tomato; lettuce; pie.

Preparation: Buy tiny bay scallops. Prepare salad and store in refrigerator. Put up potato to bake prepared as in Dinner No. 1. Figure time until rest of dinner must be started. Beans take 10 to 15 minutes; scallops, about 5. Put up water to boil; add ½ teaspoon of salt. Plunge beans into boiling water. Wash and dry scallops with paper towels. Shake in a paper or plastic bag with flour until they are evenly and thinly coated. Heat 1 tablespoon of butter and ½ tablespoon of oil in a skillet large enough to cook scallops only one layer deep. Stir frequently during cooking time, about 5 minutes. Sprinkle with lemon juice or serve with prepared tartar sauce.

Dinner No. 6

Broiled Chicken

Rice   Zucchini

Green Salad

Beer or Chilled White Wine

Coffee or Tea   Pound Cake with Frozen Strawberries

You need: one broiling chicken cut up into pieces (butcher will do this); two zucchini; one package of precooked rice; salad greens; pound cake; frozen strawberries.

Preparation: Defrost half a package of strawberries so they can be spooned over pound cake. Prepare salad and store in refrigerator. Wash chicken; cut away excess fat; dry well with paper towels. Preheat broiler. Salt and pepper chicken; brush with melted butter. Broil according to Broiling Timetable, bottom side to flame first. Determine size of rice portion from package instructions and cook accordingly. Scrub zucchini and cut into slices. Cook as per Vegetable Cooking Timetable. Drain water from zucchini and put vegetable into serving dish. Sprinkle with a little pepper, top with a pat of butter.

Dinner No. 7

Broiled Bluefish

Boiled New Potatoes   Broiled Tomato

Escarole Salad
Chilled White Wine

Coffee or Tea   Pie

You need: one bluefish split and boned; lemon; three or four potatoes; one tomato; Parmesan cheese; escarole; pie.

Preparation: Prepare salad and store in refrigerator. Scrub new potatoes. Place them in boiling water that covers potatoes. Cover pot. Cook about 20 to 40 minutes. Drain. Remove skins. (Simple! Hold potato on a fork. Skin peels off easily with paring knife.) Coat with melted butter. Sprinkle with salt and chopped parsley. Core then cut a large ripe tomato in half horizontally. Sprinkle with salt and pepper and Parmesan cheese. Broil under flame about 5 minutes. Brush fish with melted butter. Broil as per Broiling Time-table. Serve with lemon wedges.

Dinner No. 8

Flank Steak

Baked Potato   Beets

Green Salad

Red Wine

Coffee or Tea   Brownies

You need: one small flank steak; one Idaho potato; one bunch of beets; salad greens; brownies.

Preparation: Prepare salad and store in refrigerator. Prepare potato and bake as instructed on Vegetable Chart. Prepare and cook beets as per Vegetable Chart. Be sure butcher has trimmed excess fat and membrane from flank steak. Score steak with shallow crisscross slashes. Flank steak should be very close to the heat; about 2 inches. It is broiled only about 5 minutes on each side so that it cooks rare; the more well done it is, the tougher it becomes. Flank steak is carved by slicing it thinly across the grain.

Dinner No. 9

Sautéed Chicken Breasts
Boiled New Potatoes   Cauliflower
Sliced Tomato
Chilled White Wine
Coffee or Tea   Fruit

You need: one pair of boned chicken breasts; three or four small potatoes; one head of cauliflower; one tomato; fruit.

Preparation: Ask butcher to bone and remove skin from chicken breasts. You can buy boned breasts in supermarkets. Trim off excess fat. Sprinkle chicken breasts with salt and pepper. Dust lightly with flour; shake off excess. Slice tomato and set aside to serve at room temperature. Prepare and cook potatoes 20 to 40 minutes. Peel off skin; toss in melted butter, salt and pepper. Cook half a head of cauliflower as per chart. (The rest can be used the next day or eaten raw with drinks.) Melt in 2 tablespoons of butter and a drop of oil in a skillet. Place chicken breasts in skillet and saute over moderate heat. Regulate heat so butter doesn't burn. After 3 minutes, turn breasts and cook on other side for approximately same length of time. Remove meat to hot platter. To butter in skillet add lemon juice, white wine or dry vermouth. Raise heat and stir. Pour mixture over meat.

Dinner No. 10

Broiled Hamburger

Baked Potato   Sautéed Mushrooms

Sliced Tomato and Bermuda Onion Salad

Beer

Coffee or Tea   Cookies

You need: ⅓ to ½ lb. ground chuck or round steak; one Idaho potato; ¼ lb. mushrooms; tomato; Bermuda onion; cookies.

Preparation: Alternate slices of Bermuda onion and tomato, leave at room temperature. Bake potato as instructed in Dinner No. 1. Shape meat into patties 1-inch thick to which you have added ¼ teaspoon salt, a pinch of pepper plus, optionally, fresh chopped parsley and chives or sautéed onions. Wipe mushrooms off with damp cloth. Slice off ends of stems. Slice mushrooms lengthwise, including cap and stem. Melt 2 tablespoons of butter in a skillet. Add mushrooms and cook over moderate heat. Stir occasionally to insure even cooking. Mushrooms should be done in about 5 minutes. Broil hamburgers as per instructions in Broiling Timetable.

Dinner No. 11

Chicken Livers

Boiled Rice   Sauteed Mushrooms

Green Salad
Beer

Coffee or Tea   Cake

You need: six or eight chicken livers; one package pre-cooked rice; ¼ lb. mushrooms; salad greens; cake.

Preparation: Prepare salad and store in refrigerator. Wipe clean, remove veins and membrane from livers. Cut each liver in half. Be sure livers are dry. Salt and pepper liver and coat with flour. Shake off excess. Determine size of rice portion from package instructions and cook accordingly. Wipe off mushrooms with damp cloth. Slice off ends of stems; then slice lengthwise, including cap and stem. Melt 2 tablespoons of butter over moderate heat. Sauté mushrooms for a few minutes, stirring occasionally to insure even cooking. Mushrooms take about 5 minutes. In separate skillet, melt 1 tablespoon of butter over high heat. When butter is spluttering, add livers. Cook about one minute on each side. This should cook them rare. If you prefer them more well done, cook them a couple of minutes longer.

Dinner No. 12

Poached Eggs with Spinach
Green Salad
Chilled White Wine

Coffee or Tea   Fruit

You need: two eggs; one package frozen chopped spinach; salad greens; fruit.

Preparation: Prepare salad and store in refrigerator. Cook spinach as per instructions on package. Drain well in colander or sieve and place on bottom of baking dish or pie tin. Poach two eggs. When eggs are done, place on top of spinach. Sprinkle first with salt and pepper then with grated Parmesan cheese. Slide under broiler for a few minutes until cheese browns.

Dinner No. 13

Rib or Loin Lamb Chops

Baked Potato   Carrots

Chicory and Cherry Tomato Salad

Red Wine

Coffee or Tea   Pie

You need: two lamb chops; one Idaho potato; three or four carrots; chicory; cherry tomatoes; pie.

Preparation: Prepare salad and store in refrigerator. Prepare and bake potato as in Dinner No. 1. Check broiling time for lamb chops as indicated on Broiling Timetable. Figure lead time for potato before broiling chops. Prepare carrots as in Dinner No. 1, also figuring cooking time against broiling time for chops.

Dinner No. 14

Pork Chops

Apple Sauce   Baked Potato

Sliced Tomato

Beer

Coffee or Tea   Cake

You need: two pork chops about 1-inch thick; one jar of apple sauce; one Idaho potato; one tomato; cake.

Preparation: Bake potato as in Dinner No. 1. Slice tomato. Chill apple sauce which you can open at the last minute. Broil chops as per instructions in broiling chart.

Dinner No. 15

                          Broiled Salmon Steak
Chopped Spinach   Boiled New Potatoes
                              Green Salad
                          Chilled White Wine
        Coffee or Tea   Pie

You need: one salmon steak about 1-inch thick; lemon; one package frozen chopped spinach; three or four small potatoes; salad greens; pie.

Preparation: Prepare salad and store in refrigerator. Since the potatoes take the longest, put them up first. Frozen chopped spinach takes only 5 minutes. Preheat the broiler for about 10 minutes. Brush broiler rack with butter. Cooking time for fish depends on thickness of steak. Check chart for cooking time. Test for doneness with a fork. Fish flakes easily when done. Don't turn fish. When potatoes are done, peel, sprinkle with salt and pepper. Then return them to the stove over low heat for a few minutes to dry them. Toss in melted butter and chopped parsley. Serve fish with lemon wedges.

Dinner No. 16

<pre>
                    Baked Veal Chops
        Rice   Green Beans
                    Spinach Salad
                    Red Wine or Beer
    Coffee or Tea   Strawberries on Pound Cake
</pre>

You need: one veal chop about one inch thick; bread crumbs; one egg; one sliced onion; one package pre-cooked rice; ¼ lb. green beans; ¼ lb. fresh spinach; one package frozen strawberries; pound cake.

Preparation: Wash spinach and dry thoroughly. Refrigerate. Before you put dressing on salad, add a little prepared mustard to dressing and mix thoroughly. Mix ¼ cup bread crumbs, ½ teaspoon salt and a pinch of pepper. Beat an egg with a pinch of salt. Dip chop in the bread crumbs, then in the egg, then in the bread crumbs again. Heat one tablespoon of oil in a baking pan. Place chop in pan and surround with onion slices. Bake at 350 degrees for 45 minutes. Turn the chop every ten minutes so that it browns evenly. Determine size of rice portion from package instructions and cook accordingly. Figure lead time for chops. Cook green beans according to instructions on chart. Strawberries should be put out to thaw earlier. Spoon over pound cake.

Dinner No. 17

Sausage and Potatoes
Sliced Tomato
Beer
Coffee or Tea   Fruit

You need: three or four link sausages; one sliced onion; one package frozen whipped potatoes; one tomato; fruit.

Preparation: Slice tomato and leave at room temperature. Sauté sausages and onion. Prepare prepackaged frozen whipped potatoes and cook as per instructions. Mix onions and sausage into whipped potatoes and dish out onto plate.

Dinner No. 18

Broiled Ham Steak
Creamed Spinach   Baked Sweet Potato
Sliced Tomato and Spanish Onion Salad
Beer
Coffee or Tea   Fruit and Cheese

You need: one ham steak ½-inch thick; one sweet potato; one package frozen creamed spinach; one tomato; one Spanish onion; fruit and cheese.

Preparation: Slice tomato and onion and leave at room temperature. Sweet potatoes take as long to cook as Idaho potatoes. Slice off one end or puncture potato. A precooked, ready-to-eat ham slice takes only a few minutes to pan broil. Put a thin coat of oil over skillet before broiling steak. Check chart for timing. Prepare spinach as per instructions on package.

Dinner No. 19

Sautéed Smelts

Broiled Tomato   Green Beans

Green Salad

Chilled White Wine

Coffee or Tea   Ice Cream

You need: six smelts; bread crumbs; one tomato; ¼ lb. green beans; salad greens; lemon; ice cream.

Preparation: Prepare salad and store in refrigerator. Wash and dry smelts. Core tomato then cut across horizontally. Salt and pepper halves, coat with bread crumbs and dot with butter. Place under broiler flame for 5 minutes. Cook green beans as per instructions in chart. Dip smelts in bread crumbs. Melt two tablespoons of butter in skillet over moderate heat. Add smelts and cook gently, turning once, until done. This should take only a few minutes. Serve with lemon wedges.

Dinner No. 20

Sautéed Shad Roe
Baked Potato   Boiled Asparagus
Watercress Salad
Chilled White Wine or Beer
Coffee or Tea   Fruit and Cheese

You need: two roe; one Idaho potato; six to eight fat asparagus; watercress; lemon; fruit and cheese.

Preparation: Prepare salad and store in refrigerator. Wash shad roe and dry with paper toweling. Bake potato as in Dinner No. 1 and figure lead time for other dishes, all of which take very little time. Cook asparagus as per chart. Garnish with melted butter. Put a tablespoon of butter and a drop of oil in a skillet. When hot, add roe and sauté until brown on all sides. The roe splatters quite a bit, so you might put a splatter shield over the skillet to contain the grease while allowing the steam to escape. Serve with lemon wedges.

Dinner No. 21

Linguini with Pesto
Green Salad
Chilled White Wine or Beer
Coffee or Tea   Fruit

You need: one package No. 7 linguini; one can pesto; Parmesan cheese; salad greens; fruit.

Preparation: Prepare salad and store in refrigerator. Bring a large pot of water to a boil, salted at the rate of a teaspoon of salt to a quart of water. Put ⅓ of the package of linguini into water, lowering in slowly so as not to disturb the boil. Cook for about 8 minutes unless you like noodles very soft; then cook 2 or 3 minutes longer. Heat the contents of the pesto can in a saucepan. When linguini is done, immediately add cold water to halt the cooking. Drain in colander. Put linguini in a bowl, add pesto and mix thoroughly. Serve with grated Parmesan cheese.

Dinner No. 22

Steamed Soft Shell Clams
Green Salad
Beer
Coffee or Tea   Pie

You need: three dozen clams; salad greens; pie.

Preparation: Prepare salad and store in refrigerator. Scrub clams thoroughly with a vegetable brush, then put through several rinsings. Place in a pot with ½ inch of water, preferably on a rack. White wine may be substituted for water. Cook over moderate heat until clams steam open. Discard any clams that don't open. Pour broth into a bowl and serve along with another bowl of melted butter.

Dinner No. 23

Pan Broiled Calf's Liver
Baked Potato   Sautéed Spinach and Garlic
Sliced Tomato
Beer
Coffee or Tea   Fruit

You need: ½ lb. calf's liver; one Idaho potato; one chopped onion or chopped scallions; ¼ lb. fresh spinach; one tomato; fruit.

Preparation: The potato is the only thing that takes a long time, so start it well ahead. Heat a tablespoon of oil and a tablespoon of butter in a skillet. Roll liver in flour; shake off excess. Sauté about one minute on each side. Cover with chopped onion. Wash spinach. Shake off excess water. Heat a tablespoon of oil in a skillet. Add spinach and a clove of minced garlic. Cover and cook over high heat until steam appears. Lower heat and cook 5 minutes longer.

Dinner No. 24

Chili
Beer
Coffee or Tea   Cake

You need: ½ lb. ground chuck; two small chopped onions; one can kidney beans; one can tomato soup; chili powder; cake.

Preparation: Cook hamburger and a small chopped onion in a tablespoon of butter until meat is browned. Add kidney beans, ½ can undiluted tomato soup, ½ teaspoon salt, one teaspoon chili powder. Cover and simmer for a half hour. Pour into a bowl and top with chopped raw onion.

Dinner No. 25

Marinated Flank Steak
Baked Potato   Cauliflower
Cherry Tomato Salad
Red Wine
Coffee or Tea   Cake

You need: one flank steak; scallions; soy sauce; dry wine; lemon juice; one Idaho potato; one head of cauliflower; cherry tomatoes; cake.

Preparation: Since the flank steak must first soak in a marinade for a few hours, this is a good dinner for weekends when you can prepare the marinade earlier in the day. Combine three tablespoons chopped scallions, two tablespoons soy sauce, ½ cup dry red wine or dry vermouth, pinch of pepper, one tablespoon lemon juice. Pour into a dish large enough to hold the steak. Score steak in criss cross fashion on each side to prevent curling while broiling. Lay steak in marinade. Marinate steak at least two hours, turning occasionally. When you are ready to make dinner, start potato well in advance and figure lead time for broiling steak, which takes only a few minutes, and cooking cauliflower (cook only half of the cauliflower). (See charts.) Either halve tomatoes or leave whole. After broiling steak, pour any juices or marinade left in broiling pan over steak. Salt and pepper cooked cauliflower and pour melted butter over it. If you have nutmeg, put some on cauliflower.

Dinner No. 26

Broiled Lobster Tail
Baked Potato   Corn on the Cob
Green Salad
Chilled White Wine or Beer
Coffee or Tea   Ice Cream

You need: one lobster tail; lemon; one Idaho potato; one or two ears of corn; salad greens; ice cream.

Preparation: Prepare salad and refrigerate. Start baked potato. Lobster tails are usually frozen, so let them thaw. Cut away the soft underside membrane. Crack the hard upper shell. Free meat from shell then put back in to prevent curling. Preheat broiler 10 minutes. Bring pot of water for corn to a boil. Make a mixture of butter and lemon juice (about two tablespoons). Broil lobster a few inches from broiler, shell side up, for two minutes. Turn, brush meat with butter and lemon mixture and broil three more minutes. Cook corn while lobster is broiling.

Dinner No. 27

Chicken Breasts with Mushrooms
Chopped Spinach
Sliced Tomato
Chilled White Wine
Coffee or Tea   Cake

You need: one pair of chicken breasts; ¼ lb. mushrooms; one package frozen chopped spinach; one tomato; cake.

Preparation: Buy one pair of boned chicken breasts or remove bone and skin yourself. Slice tomato and set aside. Wipe breasts clean, salt and pepper and dust with flour, shaking off excess. Wipe mushrooms clean with damp cloth. Trim off ends and slice mushrooms. Heat a tablespoon of butter and a little oil in a skillet. When fat is hot but not burning add breasts. Sauté on one side for three minutes; turn and cook on other side for two minutes. Remove breasts to platter, sprinkle with salt and pepper and keep warm in oven. Add mushrooms to skillet. Add more butter if needed. Sauté mushrooms for about five minutes. If you wish, add one tablespoon of dry sherry or dry vermouth when mushrooms are done and cook over high heat to evaporate alcohol. Pour mushrooms over chicken breasts. Cook spinach according to directions on package. If you like, make a bed of spinach, place breasts on it and then mushrooms on top of that.

Dinner No. 28

Cheeseburgers

Baked Potato · · · · · · · · · · · · · · · · · · Carrots

Green Salad

Beer

Coffee or Tea · · · · · · · · · · · · · · · · · Fruit

You need: ¼ to ⅓ lb. chuck or ground round; Swiss or cheddar cheese; Idaho potato; three or four carrots; salad greens; fruit.

Preparation: Prepare and refrigerate salad. Start baked potato and figure lead time for rest of dinner. Mix meat with ¼ teaspoon of salt and a pinch of pepper. Shape into ½-inch thick patties. Place a slice of Swiss or cheddar cheese on every other patty. Cover with "uncheesed" patty and press edges together so melted cheese doesn't run out. Cook carrots as instructed in Vegetable Cooking Chart. Broil hamburgers as indicated on Broiling Chart for preferred degree of doneness.

Dinner No. 29

Broiled Filet of Sole or Lemon Sole
Green Salad
Boiled Potatoes   Green Beans
Chilled White Wine
Coffee or Tea   Fruit

You need: one large filet or two small ones; lemon; three or four medium potatoes; ¼ lb. green beans; salad greens; fruit.

Preparation: Boil potatoes as per instructions in chart. Potatoes can be left whole and doused with melted butter, salt and pepper. Pre-heat broiler for ten minutes. Brush broiler pan with butter. Place filet on pan. Salt and pepper filet lightly; dot with butter. Broil from five to seven minutes, basting with butter two or three times. Serve with lemon wedges. Cook carrots as per chart.

Dinner No. 30

Spaghetti with Clam Sauce
Escarole Salad
Chilled White Wine
Coffee or Tea   Pie

You need: one package spaghetti; one can minced clams; one clove of garlic; fresh parsley or one package of parsley flakes; olive oil; escarole; pie; Parmesan cheese.

Preparation: Prepare salad and refrigerate. Peel and chop one clove of garlic. Chop up ⅛ cup of parsley. (You can snip fresh parsley into small pieces with a scissor). If you are using dry parsley flakes, you need two teaspoonsful; soak first in water ten minutes. Heat a tablespoon of olive oil in a skillet. Sauté garlic until it turns color. Add another tablespoon of oil and the juice from a can of minced clams. Add fresh parsley or soaked parsley and its liquid and bring contents of skillet to a boil. Add the minced clams and heat thoroughly. Bring a pot of water to a boil, salted at the rate of a teaspoon of salt to a quart of water. When water boils slowly add ⅓ of the contents of a package of spaghetti slowly to water so as not to disturb boil. Cook about eight minutes, longer if you like your spaghetti soft. Add cold water to pot to stop cooking. Pour into colander and drain well. Put spaghetti into bowl and pour clam sauce over it. Sprinkle with grated Parmesan cheese.

After you've made a few of these dinners, you will begin to pick up expertise. Once you've progressed beyond the steak-and-potatoes routine, you should crack open a cookbook and start scouting around for ideas. There are literally hundreds of recipes which require little preparation and cooking time. Anybody who can read can cook.

If you were married to a good cook, try to remember some of the things she made that were particular favorites of yours. If your relationship is amicable enough, ask her for the recipes. She'll probably be more fair to you than most people are about passing on recipes. If you're a single man who just left home, ask your mother for recipes. Hopefully, she won't fight this as a final severance of the umbilical cord.

As I mentioned at the beginning of this chapter, there are many dishes you can try on weekends that can be made in quantities to last you through mid-week dinners when time is at a premium. For instance, roasts are among the easiest main dishes to cook. Pot roasts, stews, meat loaf are all more-than-one-meal dishes. They all just require time. Try them on a rainy weekend. You'll amaze yourself.

Eventually you'll want to have a few people in for drinks. You may even get the grand idea of having friends over for a housewarming.

You don't have to duplicate a liquor store's complete stock. The standards will do: scotch, bourbon, rye, gin and vodka. Stock up on mixers; club soda, ginger ale, quinine water. There are commercially prepared mixes for Bloody Marys and Old Fashioneds to which you merely add liquor and whatever fruit slices are called for. Many people prefer wine to liquor, so have some dry sherry and chilled white wine on hand. Supply dry vermouth for the martini drinkers or for those who like vermouth on the rocks.

Pick up some lemons and limes and, if you're serving Old Fashioneds, oranges. Have plenty of ice on hand. If you can't buy bags of it anywhere in your neighborhood, start making trays of ice a few days in advance and store it in your freezer.

The food part is easy. First get some cocktail-size paper napkins and toothpicks. Supermarkets carry a complete assortment of potato chips or other flavored chips, peanuts, cashews, pretzels, frozen hors d'oeuvres, cheese spreads, olives, and innumerable other edibles. Just wander up and down the aisles and fill your basket.

Of course, there's always peanut butter. People are always surprised when it's served at cocktail parties, but why not serve it? They eat peanuts. The natural peanut butter with no oils added is far superior to commercial brands. Many supermarkets stock it; health food stores certainly do.

Buy unsliced hunks of cheese: Swiss, Monterey Jack, cheddar, Roquefort or any of the bleu cheeses. If there's a cheese store in your neighborhood or if a local department store has a food department, you can increase your selection. Most cheese stores will let you taste before you buy. Place the cheese on a platter with knives along with a basket of unsalted crackers or sliced French bread.

Raw vegetables are a snap. Slice carrots, green pepper, celery, fennel, turnip. Buy scallions, radishes, cauliflower, or cherry tomatoes. You can gussy it up with a dip. Mix a little curry powder into prepared mayonnaise. Blend cream cheese and chopped chives with a little sour cream. Or just put out the salt and pepper.

Buy a salami and slice it. Toothpicks and mustard complete the dish. Same with baked ham. If you live in a city with a good French bakery, ask if they make *quiche Lorraine*, a delicious cheese and bacon pie. You only have to warm it up and serve slices or let people take their own. If there's an Italian grocery available, buy a selection of Italian cured meats, olives, and salads and serve a platter of antipasto.

Supermarkets carry packaged pre-sliced party breads. They come in pumpernickel or rye. These breads are much smaller in circumference than regular breads. They're fine for cheese, sliced meats, or, even, raw vegetables.

Fish markets sell cleaned and cooked shrimp. Be prepared to pay dearly for this, since they've done all the work for you. You can buy prepared cocktail sauces at supermarkets or fish markets. Just supply toothpicks. Smoked fish, such as Nova Scotia, whitefish, and herrings are generally expensive but work-free. Herrings packed in wine sauce, brine or sour cream merely require transferring contents of jar to bowl.

Don't put out too much. If you are four people, a bowl of peanuts, a couple of cheeses and a dish of raw vegetables are sufficient. Or you can substitute salami or herring for the vegetables.

Once you've had people over for cocktails, you'll gain courage for the next step: inviting someone over for dinner. A bachelor has one built-in advantage. People expect little. In fact, they're downright wary that they might be flirting with gastrointestinal trauma. So you're ahead if they consider the meal merely edible.

After they've cooked a few simple meals, many men become intrigued with cooking. You may turn out to be one of them. Give it a try. If at first you don't succeed, remember: drug stores are stocked with antacids.

6
Manning the Dustcloth and Other General Housekeeping Exercises

I would expect Women's Liberationists to rebel less against being used as sex objects than against the slave labor known as housework. Housework is unrelieved, repetitive tedium with no reward. Surely many a woman has departed this earth sighing, "Well, at least I'm through with housework."

But clean we must. In a small town or in the country, it's less of a chore. The air is generally cleaner and things just don't get as dirty as often. If, however, you live in the city, you are often surrounded by modern industries which pump money into the economy at the cost of pumping soot into the air. Most of it seems to land on your furniture.

If you can afford to have a cleaning person come in at least once a week, your life as a single man will be immeasurably sweetened. If you can afford to have someone come in more often, you may never miss a woman around the house.

Day-to-day cleaning chores consist mostly in transferring dust from your furniture and window sills to a rag, from the floor to a mop, or in sucking up floor debris with a vacuum cleaner.

Let's assume you are hard pressed for cash and must do the housework yourself. You'll probably do most of it on the weekend. Like any other job, it is much easier if you organize some sort of routine. And, obviously, having the proper equipment makes the job easier. In general, good quality cleaning tools, carefully selected, more than pay for themselves in the time and energy they save you.

Cleaning Tools

Dust cloths   These go under the inelegant name of "rags." Rags come from old shirts, old undershirts, towels, tablecloths, etc. Undershirts make the best rags because of their soft knit construction. You can buy commercially packaged cloths of synthetics, cotton, flannel and other materials. Many of these are chemically treated to help with polishing. Most are washable.

Sponges   Cellulose sponges are sold in supermarkets and hardware stores. They come in various sizes. They are excellent for washing tile, woodwork, formica, and floors.

Chamois   An oil tanned sheepskin that is excellent for windows. It polishes as it cleans.

Dustpan and brush   Used for sweeping up small areas, as under a table, or for gathering debris you have swept together in a pile.

Broom   Fiber brooms are more satisfactory and more durable than straw ones. Store with fiber end up or hang from a hook in the broom closet. Storing it with the fibers resting on the floor eventually breaks the fibers.

Mops   You need a dry mop for dusting the floor. This must be washed out occasionally. You also need a wet mop for the bathroom and kitchen floors or any other tiled floors. Don't buy the old-fashioned string type. Get a mop with a replaceable cellulose head or sponge. It comes with a clamp arrangement for squeezing out excess water. You can easily wash it out for reuse.

Water pail   Galvanized tin or plastic, with handle.

Rubber gloves

Floor brush   For sweeping up the bare floors of debris heavier than just dust.

Carpet sweeper   Even if you have a vacuum cleaner, this is essential for quick clean-ups when you don't want to go through hooking up the vacuum cleaner.

Vacuum cleaner and attachments   The general all-around work horse for removing dirt from floors, rugs, furniture, walls, etc. Buy a good one.

Electric floor polisher   (Optional) This buffs floors and polishes. The heavier the machine, the better the polishing job. Some home models are too light to do an adequate job. The wax can be spread by hand with a rag or with a lamb's wool applicator. Wood floors need infrequent waxing. In between, buffing keeps them looking great.

Toilet brush and container   Self-explanatory. This job gets done about once a week. The bowl often tends to stain from the water standing in it. There is a bowl cleaner on the market with disposable cellulose pads which fit onto a handle.

Cleaning Supplies

Read the instructions on labels of all cleaning supplies. You'll get pertinent information you need for usage, generally will be warned about limitations and dangers, cautioned about edibility and suddenly discover that today's housekeeping can be considerably lightened by a doctorate in chemistry.

Detergents   Regular laundry detergents can do some jobs for you.

Heavy duty, extra-strong detergents, either liquid or powder, are made especially for household cleaning.

Scouring powder   Abrasives that are used for cleaning tile, sinks, pots and other similar hard surfaces.

Dishwashing detergent   There are special detergents for machines; others, for sinks or dishpans.

Ammonia   A general all-purpose cleaner.

Metal polish   Self-explanatory. Be sure it can be used on the metal surfaces you have. Chrome, for instance, can be cleaned with just warm soapy water. Metal polish, unless specified on the label, may remove chrome finishes.

Steel wool   For scouring pots and pans. Finer grades can be used for cleaning stubborn spots off of floors.

Plastic scouring pads   For scrubbing surfaces which would be damaged if attacked with steel wool.

Furniture polish   This includes lemon oil, which is fine for some wood finishes. Polishes come in liquid, cream, paste and spray-on. This, too, is not a weekly chore, unless your mother's coming over. There are spray polishes on the market which you apply as you dust.

Floor waxes   There are two types of floor waxes—buffing and self-polishing. The self-polishing waxes, a water-emulsion formula, require little work and are therefore more desirable. They are used on composition floors, such as linoleum, vinyl, asphalt, on ceramic tile and on varnished wooden floors. They dry to a shine without buffing. Buffing waxes, paste and liquid cleaning and polishing formulas are primarily for wooden floors. They must be spread on the floor and then buffed. The extra work they require explains the popularity of wall-to-wall carpeting.

Store these items in the cabinet under your kitchen sink. You can increase the storage space by putting a shelf under the sink or by using the same stacking bins you use for storing vegetables. Either of these items can be purchased in a housewares or hardware store.

Once you have assembled your cleaning equipment and supplies, the next thing to add is *YOU.*

There are only three cleaning jobs that have to be attacked with any regularity: dusting, dry mopping the floors, and cleaning around the kitchen and bathroom. Even that depends on your own standards—or lack of them. Men who live in the city are faced with a fresh supply of soot delivered daily, free of charge. If you live in one of the newer, centrally air-conditioned and heated buildings, windows can be kept sealed so that no dirt or "fresh" air sullies your living quarters.

But, assume you open your windows. With a soft cloth dust all window sills, flat surfaces, and objects resting on these surfaces, such as books you haven't moved in a week.

After dusting, if you don't take time off to rest, wipe up the floors with the dry mop. Check the area under the dining table for scraps of food that never made it to your mouth. Many people consider dogs excellent for this type of clean-up detail. However, dogs create more than enough dirt on their own to offset their substitution for a vacuum cleaner. If you're going to keep a dog, do it because you love him, not because he'll help you clean.

The kitchen can be kept moderately clean if you spend a few minutes after cooking wiping up with a damp sponge. Floor spills, spatters on the stove, the sink—all can be wiped clean in seconds.

The bathroom can be kept reasonably sanitary with the same kind of quick-wipe remedy. Save the big cleaning for once a week. An excellent way to keep your bathroom clean is to join a local gym or "Y" where you will do all your showering. This way the tub only gets dusty. Apply a coat of liquid wax to tile surfaces. It prevents soap scum from forming on the tile. You just wipe clean with a damp cloth. You occasionally have to renew the wax surface.

Even if you decide to ignore minimal cleaning during the week, you are eventually faced with the decision to clean or move. Let's assume you opt for only weekly cleaning. During the week you have settled for making the bed (maybe) and shoving aside any debris that gets in your way—or even for just blowing the dust off a book or magazine you laid down a few days ago.

Making a bed with contour bottom sheets often is as difficult as slipping a sweater on an octopus. It's infinitely easier if you put the sheet on diagonally opposite corners first, one at the head of the mattress, one at the foot. Then the other two will go on much more easily.

On a weekly basis you should dust, dry mop the floors, run the vacuum over the rugs, damp mop the bathroom and kitchen floors, clean out the toilet bowl, bathtub and sink and—if you can push yourself a bit further—spread self-polishing wax on the bathroom and kitchen floors. Incidentally, many people use commercial deodorizers in the bathroom. In the summer this may be all right, but in the winter heating often intensifies the masking odor. You can deodorize quickly and cheaply with matches. Keep a book of them handy in the bathroom.

On a less frequent basis, you should wipe down the baseboards and woodwork. Wipe off lampshades, picture frames, radiators, light fixtures. If, when you look out the windows, you think you are living in perpetual twilight, you might find it's time to wash the windows. For window cleaning you can use warm water diluted with a little ammonia, or any of the commercial spray preparations available. Crumpled newspaper is excellent for wiping windows clean. So is chamois. If cobwebs have formed in corners, don't regard them as an original decorating idea. Remove them with a rag tied around a broom, dry mop, or stick.

Occasionally remove books from the shelves, dust both the books and the shelves. If you have venetian blinds, one of the most efficient dust collectors ever invented, wipe them off with warm soapy water.

The whole routine of devoting part of your weekends to intensive cleaning is depressing enough to send you back to mother. You could schedule yourself for light housekeeping only and decide to do one room thoroughly each weekend.

Many new refrigerators are now self-defrosting. If you don't have this kind, eventually your freezer compartment develops a snowy covering similar to the polar ice cap. It affects the efficiency of the machine. This is corrected by turning the refrigerator control to "Defrost" or "Off" and adjusting the tray under the freezer to catch melting ice. If the tray has a plug, remove it and place a pot on the first shelf directly under the drainage hole to catch the water. If not, the tray full of water is tricky to carry to the sink without spilling. One way to beat this, assuming you have only enough ice to fill the tray once, is to leave the water in the tray after defrosting; turn the refrigerator back on. An ice film will form. Lift out the tray and discard its contents.

When you decide to defrost, first remove everything from the freezer. When you anticipate a defrosting, try first to use up the contents of the freezer. After the ice has melted, wipe out the interior of the freezer and refrigerator compartment, refill the ice trays, and turn the controls back to the proper setting. Incidentally, if your refrigerator doesn't have a built-in thermometer, buy one. It's a safety measure to insure proper storage temperature.

If you have been using your oven for broiling or roasting, you should clean it out occasionally. There are commercial solvents which can be bought in supermarkets. You need rubber gloves and dedication for this job. You can avoid part of this job by soaking the broiler rack and tray in soapy water every time you use it. It cleans easily. Then you only have to clean the slotted grooves in the broiler section of the oven.

By now you should begin to see why many people are willing to sacrifice other comforts in order to be able to afford a cleaning person.

Once in a while, run the vacuum over your mattress to get rid of accumulated dust.

There are some seasonal cleaning chores which are optional. These include sending off heavy winter blankets for cleaning and storage during warm months. Obviously, you send off light blankets for the same purposes in cold weather.

If you have drapes, remove them during the summer and have them cleaned and stored. In hot weather, with windows open, they collect more dust. Besides, they make the room look warmer. Curtains also need occasional cleaning. If your floors are covered with heavy wool rugs, clean them and either store them or roll them up and slide them under the bed or behind the sofa during summer. Bare floors look cooler. If you can afford it, buy small, flat, inexpensive scatter rugs for summer.

The change of seasons is also the time to wipe out closets. You can do this with rags or with your vacuum.

Now that you have learned the secrets of tedious toil, we can turn to one housekeeping chore which you face almost daily: washing dishes.

One way to eliminate dishwashing is a hunger strike. If you have a dishwasher, your problems are minimal. You don't have to run the machine after every meal. Just rinse off the dishes and stack them in the washer until the machine is full. Then run it. You then only have to wash a pot or two.

Don't, however, put knives into a dishwasher unless they are made of a single piece of metal. When blades are attached to handles by some sort of glue, they eventually loosen.

If you don't have a dishwasher, there are ways of cutting down the onerous task of doing dishes by hand (other than eating with paper plates). Soak them in warm, soapy water with the flatware on the bottom. This removes most of the grease and loosens more stubborn dirt. Then you merely have to rub them a bit with a soapy sponge or cloth, rinse them off, and let them drain. Warm water is best for washing, except for eggs, fish, and dough. For these, use cold water.

Drying dishes is optional. If you have room to let them drain dry, do so. If you are cramped for space, let them drain a bit so that most of the water runs off. Drying is then easier.

Most pots and pans need just warm soapy water to get them clean. Let them soak in this mixture while you are eating, and cleaning will be easier. If, however, pots or pans are covered with sticky or charred residue that doesn't rinse off, use steel wool and scouring powder, then rinse. Don't use steel wool on enamel coated, Teflon, or glass cookware. If you own a blender, a quick way to clean it is to fill it with hot water. Add a few drops of dishwashing lotion, then turn the machine on for a few seconds. Rinse it out with clean water.

There's only one other area of housekeeping you face with regularity: laundry. How often you do laundry is regulated by how quickly you run out of clean underwear. Assume it's a weekly chore.

There are three ways you can get your laundry done. You can send everything to a commercial laundry along with your shirts and sheets. This is the most expensive solution. You can take it to a laundromat. There are two kinds of laundromats. In one, you load your machine and wait until your laundry is done. Then throw it into a dryer and wait. In the other, you drop off your laundry and pick it up later all washed, dried, and roughly folded. There is often a small surcharge for this service. Laundromats that do your laundry for you often supply detergent, bleach, and fabric softener; in others, you bring your own. The least expensive and time-consuming method is your own machine or machines located in the basement of your apartment house.

In New York City, the laundry circuit is an established method for meeting new people. Once they have exhausted the social possibilities of their own laundry rooms, many bachelors cart their laundry to neighboring buildings in quest of new liaisons.

For doing laundry you need detergent or soap, bleach, and fabric softener. The detergent or soap washes out soil, bleach whitens, and fabric softener returns to the fabric suppleness and softness that is removed by detergent. Follow package instructions. Too much detergent means too much suds, which can clog the machine and cause a breakdown. Too much bleach can weaken fabrics as well as remove color along with stains.

If your laundry load is big enough, separate whites from colored fabrics. Only machine-wash colors that are colorfast. Colorfast means the dye won't run. If a fabric is not colorfast, the dye may stain other items washed in the same load.

If anything is badly soiled, soak it in a soapy solution for a few hours overnight prior to machine washing. Some people throw socks in with the rest of the laundry. This is easier, but, unfortunately, the socks too often become covered with lint. Decide for yourself whether this bothers you. If it does, wash your socks by hand.

Ironing should be minimal. About the only thing you may be faced with pressing is handkerchiefs. A trick for avoiding this is to press the wet handkerchief against the tiled bathroom walls or tub. After they dry, peel them off and fold. It's assumed you sent your shirts and bed linen to a commercial laundry. If you own permanent press, no-iron bed linen of percale or cotton and synthetic blend, you can machine wash, dry in dryer, fold, and store away.

If anything you own is labeled "drip dry" or "wash-and-wear," do exactly that. Wash it, hang it up sopping wet, and smooth out the fabric to eliminate any wrinkling. Hang jeans or pants upside down, pulling pocket lining out (four layers of cloth take longer to dry than two). The heavier weight of the top of the pants will pull them tauter so they'll dry smoother.

By now you have become an expert housekeeper. It is my guess that if most divorced men were required to read this chapter prior to divorce, they would try harder for reconciliation. After all, it may not have been the best relationship, but at least the place was clean —and you probably didn't have to do anything about it.

7

The Care and Feeding
of Your Wardrobe

Did you ever notice how many women you see in a men's clothing department? It has nothing to do with unisex. Many wives go along with their husbands when they're out to buy new suits or sports jackets. There are a couple of reasons. One is that he honestly values her judgment and is dressing to please her. The other is that she's wary of his taste and may not be sure whom he is dressing to please.

The scene in the men's furnishings departments is even more singular. Here you will find the wife buying her husband's shirts, socks, pajamas, and underwear without the man along even for consultation. His approval of her choices is taken for granted. This doesn't necessarily mean the man is hen-pecked; he just doesn't want to be bothered. The same scenario is repeated by mothers who keep their sons' stock of furnishings replenished.

So you have a lot of men who actually can't tell you what size socks they wear. If you're single, be sure to ask mom. How can a man go out on his own and stand on his own two feet if his socks are too tight? If you're a married man who fits into this category and you're about to part from your personal professional shopper, check her for your sizes before you reach the not-talking-to-each-other stage. It's not the type of information you pass on to one another through your lawyers. Imagine a wife saying, "Tell him that if he agrees with my figures for monthly alimony, I'll tell him what size underwear he wears."

Even if you did all your own shopping while married, you certainly spent little time taking care of your clothes. Perhaps your total contribution was a "Honey, will you send my blue pinstriped suit to the cleaners?"

In the course of the disintegration of your marriage, you probably first dropped the "Honey" and later she told you to take the damned suit to the cleaners yourself. If so, you at least were pushed into the first step in learning how to take care of your own wardrobe.

The care and maintenance of clothing is one of the simplest jobs you'll have. Clothes are generally either washed by hand or in a machine or they are dry-cleaned. Some items, like hats, survive for years with just occasional brushing. Ties kept free of stains can spend their entire lifetime with no care on your part. If you do spot a tie, you're in trouble. Few dry cleaners handle ties expertly.

The previous chapter covered instructions on how to do laundry and how to handle wash-and-wear items. You should know that any spot stands a better chance of being removed the sooner you attack it. *Cold* water applied immediately will remove many stains. *Hot* water sets stains.

The most common stain removers are water, kerosene, denatured alcohol, carbon tetrachloride, petroleum jelly, turpentine, white talcum powder, cornstarch, bleach, glycerine, and salt. And there are spray spot removers which absorb grease and dry to a white powder. You simply brush off the powder. If you are uncertain about the fabric's reaction to a stain remover, test it on a hidden part of the garment, such as an inside seam flap.

Water is usually the most effective stain remover. If the material is washable, soaking will often remove the stain. If the material is non-washable and you want to soak it, be sure the water won't remove the color as well as the stain or leave its own stain.

Here are some common stains and recommended ways of removing them.

Acids   (Citrus, perspiration, urine, vinegar); treat immediately. Rinse or sponge with cold water; then neutralize the acid with diluted ammonia water (10 percent solution) applied to both sides of the fabric. Hold the moistened stain over an opened ammonia bottle so that it can absorb the fumes that often restore color.

Adhesive tape   Sponge with carbon tetrachloride.

Alcohol or soft drinks   Sponge with denatured alcohol.

Blood   Sponge or wash in cold or lukewarm water. If the material is washable, soak the stain in cold water until it turns light brown; then wash in warm soapy water. If stain has dried, add 2 tablespoons of ammonia water (10 percent solution) per gallon of water to the soaking water.

Candle wax   Crumble off excess then place between clean white blotters and press with warm iron. Change blotters as they soil. Then sponge with carbon tetrachloride.

Chewing gum   Sponge with carbon tetrachloride until gum softens. Then pick off with fingers. You can also freeze it by pressing an ice cube against it; then pick it off.

Chocolate   First scrape off as much as possible with a dull knife. If the material is washable, wash in warm soapy water. If not, sponge with carbon tetrachloride, then sponge with warm water.

Coffee or tea   If material is washable, pour boiling water through stain from reverse side of fabric, then wash in warm soapy water. If stain persists, bleach with hydrogen peroxide. If material is not washable (wool or silk), sponge with lukewarm water, then rub glycerine over it lightly between your hands. Let stand a half hour, then rinse thoroughly with water. If grease spot from milk or cream remains, sponge with carbon tetrachloride.

Eggs   Sponge with cold water. If stain persists, sponge with carbon tetrachloride.

Fruit (except peach)   Sponge with warm water. If stain persists, sponge with cold water, rubbing in a little glycerine. Let stand 3 hours, swab with vinegar, rinse with water.

Grass   If material is not washable, sponge with denatured alcohol. If material is washable, rub stain well with hot water and soap. If this isn't successful, use a bleach.

Gravy   Wet down with carbon tetrachloride. If stain remains, apply lukewarm water.

Grease   If material isn't washable, sponge with carbon tetrachloride or other grease solvent. Hold a blotter or soft cloth under cloth to absorb stain. If material is washable, make a soap paste, smear it on stain and soak in cold water.

Ink   If material is not washable, try water. If this doesn't work, try an absorbent powder. For washable materials, rub with glycerine and rinse in cold water.

Lipstick   For non-washable materials, first soften by rubbing in vaseline or lard. Sponge non-washable materials with carbon tetrachloride. If stain still persists, rub with denatured alcohol. For acetate or colored materials, dilute the alcohol, one part alcohol to two parts water. For washable materials, first rub in petroleum jelly or glycerine then wash.

Mustard   For non-washables, apply warm glycerine and sponge with water. For washables, rub in glycerine or soap, then wash with soap and water.

Paint   Place stain down on blotter or on pad of soft material. Apply soft soap jelly on reverse side until stain works out. If stain persists, apply turpentine. Washable materials may be sponged or immersed in turpentine.

Rust   Sponge with lemon juice and salt.

Shoe polish   Sponge with carbon tetrachloride or denatured alcohol.

Soot   Sponge non-washables with carbon tetrachloride or gasoline. Sprinkle washables with an absorbent powder then wash with soap and water.

Tar   For non-washable materials, soften with petroleum jelly then sponge with carbon tetrachloride.

Tobacco   For non-washable materials, sponge with cold water, then apply lukewarm water and glycerine. If this doesn't remove stain, sponge it with denatured alcohol. For washables, sponge with cold water, work warm glycerine into the stain, let stand a half hour, then wash with soap and water.

Urine   Sponge with warm water with a few drops of ammonia added. Let it stand 15 minutes then rinse with clear water.

Wine   Apply salt as soon as the stain occurs.

Too much dry cleaning harms many fabrics. Most garments will survive a season's wear with occasional brushing to remove surface soil. Keep a good, moderately stiff clothes brush handy and every once in a while brush your suits, jackets, slacks, or coats before you hang them away in the closet. Don't hang something dirty in your closet and forget it. Perspiration, body soil, and other dirt can shorten the life of a garment. Get it cleaned as soon as possible.

Good wooden hangers that widen at the ends to support the shoulder construction of your jackets and coats help keep your clothes looking better longer. Wire hangers are not sturdy enough. Crowding clothes in the closet creases them and prevents ventilation. Shoe trees keep your shoes in shape longer. Keep your sweaters on shelves. Even heavy sweaters will stretch if left on hangers.

Most men are vaguely aware of the day-to-day care of their clothes. But the change of seasons sets into motion a routine which wives and mothers supervise and husbands and sons take for granted. As warm weather approaches, your lighter-weight garments appear from somewhere as heavy ones disappear. As the cooler weather approaches, the situation reverses itself.

Let's take the changeover from winter to spring and summer first. When the tweeds feel even more itchy, it's time to put them away. Send all your heavy woolen coats, slacks, and suits to the dry cleaner. If you have no room to store them in your apartment, you can store them at the dry cleaner for a nominal charge. If you store them at the dry cleaner, be sure he doesn't press the garments until he is ready to return them to you.

If you have enough room to store your clothes at home, be sure your closets are roomy enough to hang garments freely without jamming them on top of one another. A slightly more expensive method of storing at home is to have them cleaned only but not pressed until you're ready to wear them. For some reason, dry cleaners charge more if you separate these two jobs. Hang the clothes in your closet covered with the plastic covers in which the cleaner delivers them. If you don't have covers, put the clothes in garment bags. If the cleaner stuffs the sleeves of your jackets and coats with tissue paper, leave it in. It helps retain the shape of the sleeve and reduces creasing.

A garment which you have worn only a couple of times during the season and haven't spotted doesn't have to be dry-cleaned. Give it a good brushing and hang it away.

Be sure to dry-clean mufflers too. They pick up soil and perspiration and oil from your neck and hair. Brush your hats off well and return them to their original boxes (if you saved them). If you're putting away shoes, wipe them clean first, then shine them to protect the leather.

Sweaters can be either washed or dry-cleaned. Washing is a complicated procedure in which you must not only wash the sweater, you must block it so it retains its original size and shape, assuming you will do the same. Who needs it? Have your sweaters dry-cleaned.

Don't store away anything that is not clean. In the fall, you may find that a stain is gone only because the moths removed it along with the material.

Hang moth preventive cakes in your closets. This reduces the chances of error and also helps prevent mildew during damp, rainy months. Also place camphor in drawers with woolens that are stored away. Don't go too heavy on the camphor. If your clothes reek of camphor when you start wearing them again, you not only chase away the moths, people avoid you.

The change from summer to winter is mostly a reversal of the same routine. Many summer suits are wash-and-wear or washable and can be handled by your laundry. This applies to all cotton slacks, jackets, and shorts, as well as cottons combined with synthetics.

Obviously there's more to the change of seasons than just bird migrations.

The one area where you may run into trouble is mending. You do as little as possible, if any at all. Most dry cleaners will accommodate you on small mending jobs if you point it out to them. Big tears in woolens often require reweaving. This is an expensive process, so you have to decide whether the cost is warranted by the anticipated service from the garment.

If you wear a hole in your socks, throw them away. Darning is for experts. A good practice in buying socks is to always buy at least two identical pairs. If one sock goes, you can still match it up with the other pair.

The only mending problem you may face from time to time is sewing on a button. Commercial laundries have employees who specialize in removing buttons from shirts before they are returned to you. If the laundry does sew the button on, it is usually too large for the buttonhole.

One way to solve this problem is to get friendly with some lady who knows how to sew on buttons. Invite her up to dinner. After she's suffused with wine and your good cooking and revelling in fantasies of being violated, drag out the shirts, needle, thread, and buttons and let her play house. (Let me know if it works!)

8
Entertaining Your Children

Visiting rights mark the first time many men are really with their children. It's the rare man who has been alone with his offspring. Usually his time with them was spent watching TV or doing some chore while the kids were playing, during the time his wife was out having her hair done. Most of his previous outings were, maybe, half-a-day; more infrequently, a full day. But when he got home, someone else took over the feeding, bathing, consoling, and getting ready for bed.

During the work week, your contact with the children may have been limited solely to dinner. Commuters often miss out on this dubious pleasure. Now that you are suddenly single, when the kids visit it's suddenly your job.

Visiting rights are usually set by court order. You and your wife may have worked out an arrangement mutually agreeable and best for the children. In some cases, the father moves too far away for frequent visits. Or the wife may have moved away, taking the children with her. If this happens, write and send picture postcards frequently. Call as often as you can afford. Try to arrange long weekends so that you can see them frequently throughout the year. Plan to spend time with them during their Christmas or Easter school vacations. Perhaps you can take them on a trip with you during summer vacation.

Try to make your visits predictable; that is, let them be set according to a definite schedule. This makes it easier for both you and their mother to make plans. Plus it makes the children feel more secure—they can look forward to each visit. This doesn't mean you can't have spontaneous visits, as long as they are not too disruptive to the children's regular routine. For example, you can decide quite suddenly to take them to an early dinner. Of course, this assumes that your relationship with their mother isn't too unpleasant. Otherwise, she might resent your "busting in" when the mood pleases you.

In fact, it pays to make a special effort to keep the lines of communication open between you and your wife so that changes in plans don't become an excuse for anger and upheaval that burden the children and increase their anxiety. It's also easier on you.

Above all, don't think you'll make it easier if you step out of the picture so that the children will then not be torn by competing loyalties. They can only interpret such action on your part as meaning you don't love them, and there is nothing worse. If you have specific problems about the children, it might best be taken up with a professional (but definitely not with any of your friends who have children and therefore "understand").

It may also help to read a good book. Ask your local library. If they can't recommend anything, here are a few books you can select from: Haim Ginott's *Between Parent and Child* and *Between Parent and Teenager*. Public Affairs Pamphlets (381 Park Avenue South, New York, N. Y. 10016) publishes many helpful pamphlets dealing with children. The Children's Bureau, Washington, D.C. also has much helpful material. Your children's pediatrician may also have some helpful suggestions.

In the beginning, the visits may be awkward for both of you. Your children are in a strange place. This is where Daddy lives. It's different from where Daddy used to live. So, your first job is to make them feel at ease. Have room for them to sleep overnight, even if it's only a sleeping bag. If they have one, suggest they bring it with them. Give them a place to put their clothes instead of making them live out of a suitcase. This will help them feel that your home is their home when they visit you.

Find out what foods they like to eat besides candy and french fried potatoes. Hopefully, you don't have to be told to try to maintain their normal eating habits. Don't turn their visit into a gastronomic orgy of ice cream and popcorn.

If you feel guilty about what the divorce has done to the kids, don't try to assuage your feelings by plying them with presents or being a tour guide to every event that's in town. They're your kids and they don't have to be bought off. They're ready to be loved. Besides, it will make them suspicious. That doesn't mean you shouldn't exercise normal discipline. You're the father, not a doting grandparent with privileges to spoil the child. Nor are you their pal.

As a general rule, it's a good idea to have plans for their visit, but be ready to chuck them. You may find they don't want the distraction of outside entertainment. They may just want to be with you and do simple things like take a walk or talk about problems on their minds. In fact, even when you have a planned activity that the children agree to, leave time for being together and talking. If one of the kids has a birthday, plan something special.

Teenagers are a special problem. If you have a teenage daughter, it's nice to take her to lunch sometimes or, if it's available, the theatre. Both boy and girl teenagers enjoy sporting events. This is a great way to spend your time and provides an enjoyable experience you can share later on. You can also talk to each other while it's going on, which makes it an improvement over the movies.

Don't take kids who are too young to ballgames because they get bored and you get angry. If you can stand the fact that all they want to do is eat popcorn and drink soft drinks and look around and really pay no attention to what's happening on the field, that's okay.

What success you have with the older children will depend very much on what kind of relationship you have already developed with them. The less there has been, the more difficult it will be to find activities the child will want to share with you and you may have to work a little harder at it. If you don't have a good relationship, the teenager is more likely to want a friend along than the younger child. The teenager will also do more balking because he or she is beginning to have his or her own social life out of the home. It will be difficult for them to admit to you that they would rather be with their friends or go to a party than be with you. If you can be flexible, it will help the growth of your own relationship with them.

I assume you have the good sense not to tell the children what a witch their mother is. After all, they have to go back to her. And while they shouldn't meet every woman you're dating, they should meet someone about whom you are serious. Wait till they tell Mommy about *her*!

Now, how can you spend your time with them?

First, don't do anything you yourself hate to do. If you're bored or restless, the kids will pick it up and it will spoil any pleasure you had hoped for. Choose things you all like. After all, the whole purpose is to enjoy yourselves together. You're their father, not a baby sitter. Don't restrict yourself to activities where you are merely spectators. Initiate projects in which you work with the children—in which you are both involved in doing something together.

Activities with children fall roughly into two categories: those you can do at home, those done away from home.

Two excellent paperback books filled with ideas for amusing children are *838 Ways to Amuse a Child* by June Johnson and *Making Things* by Ann Wiseman. Both rely heavily on materials you either have around the house or can easily obtain.

Activities at Home

Games You may already know games they like to play. If not, buy a couple at a toy store. Or ask them to bring their favorites along with them. Older kids might like Monopoly. There are card games for all ages. It's far preferable to choose games that are not fiercely competitive; the more non-competitive, the better. If the games are ones in which you participate, try to have games in which you don't have to cheat to lose.

Jigsaw puzzles   These range from extremely simple ones for small children to more complex ones you can solve with them.

Blocks   This is for the younger ones. Blocks doesn't mean just A, B, C blocks. There are building blocks with which they can erect simple constructions.

Construction toys   This includes log cabin sets and various wood and plastic sets with which kids can build real and fantasy constructions.

Model kits   This is for the older children. There are kits for airplanes, ships, automobiles, trains, and various other items. Don't buy too much, because storage of the models becomes a problem and you probably don't have that much room.

Drawing and painting   Supply crayons, finger paints, or water colors plus paper. You can make your own finger paint, from chocolate pudding.

Reading to them   This is obviously for the younger ones. They can bring along their favorite story books or you can buy a couple of new ones. A bookstore can probably suggest some titles. If the children read themselves and enjoy it, it's nice to set aside some time for you each to read your own books.

Storytelling   Also for the little ones. You may have to do some background reading of children's fairy tales or similar fare.

Watching TV   There may be some programs you both enjoy, like sporting events. They can watch their own programs while you're making dinner. Guard against using TV as a cop-out because you can't think of anything to do. Don't let it become a time-killing anesthetic.

Making dinner together   Let them help you set the table or do whatever chores they're old enough to handle.

Entertaining Your Children   127

Baking   There are all sorts of very easy frozen and ready-mix cake doughs.

Letting them make a dinner they've planned   Very big with little girls who feel there's a void in your life that they must fill by playing "mother." However, don't let this get out of hand so the kid ends up feeling sorry for poor you.

Making popcorn   You can buy self-contained units which are aluminum pans with the corn already inside. All you do is put it over a stove burner. You can also buy canned or jarred dry corn which you can pop in a covered skillet.

Making fudge   A little more work but not difficult. Just fattening.

Playing records   Here too they can bring their own or you can have some around. It's also an opportunity to introduce them to music.

Making a fire in your fireplace   You can add to this pleasure by popping corn or, if possible, grilling franks or hamburgers over the fire.

Helping with homework   This is something you should offer to do but pick your subjects carefully. How much algebra do you remember?

Clay modeling   Clay is easily available at craft shops or toy stores. You can teach them to make simple ashtrays, candle holders, bowls.

Soap carving   This assumes you are reasonably dexterous. For little kids your simplest efforts will be masterpieces.

Papier-mâché modeling

Wood whittling   Here too you need a little expertise.

Indoor gardening   You can have some house plants that they take care of on their visits. You might put together a terrarium with them. In the spring, consider seed flats for flowering plants that can grow in the house. An avocado plant started from a pit is fun to watch grow.

Knot tying   Knots for sailors, mountain climbing, package tying, etc. All are a lot of fun.

Macramé   Kits are available in toy stores, craft shops and some variety stores.

Astronomy kits   If they become interested, you can combine this with nighttime sky watching. You can teach them (or they, you) how to identify stars, planets and constellations.

Aquariums   If you want to take this on, they can be fascinated by the goings-on in an aquarium. You can shop for the fish together, set up the aquarium, and maintain it together. Just remember, you're the gamekeeper when they're not there.

Making sponge animals   You cut cellulose sponges into pieces resembling animal parts; then you cement the pieces together.

Collages   A collage is a picture made of small sections of many pictures; other materials may be added. Pick a theme such as a vacation, animals, airplanes, etc.

Making jewelry   Make beads of macaroni, dough balls, or spools.

Mobiles   A mobile is a free-hanging design that moves with the breeze. You can suspend it from a wire hanger.

Constructing doll houses or forts   Cardboard cartons or shoe boxes provide excellent material for these constructions.

Building a scrapbook on a favorite subject   Leaves or flowers collected on walks, animals, airplanes are some of the subjects you can choose.

Photography   If you have the space and the money for developing equipment, this makes it even more interesting.

Finger puppets or hand puppets

Making a puppet theatre   This provides a place in which you can put your puppets to work.

Beadwork   You can buy kits for this in craft shops or good toy stores.

Making candles

Making tin can lanterns   You simply perforate the can with a design and put a candle inside.

Making bread dough sculptures

Tie-dying or batik dying

Constructing a skate scooter to use outdoors

Making stocking masks

Activities away from Home

Movies   Be sure you understand the rating system.

Bowling   Even little ones who can just about lift the bowling ball enjoy this. Besides, it's your one chance to perhaps win a game.

Sports events   Football, baseball, hockey, basketball, horse shows, dog shows.

Eating in restaurants   If money is a problem, Chinese restaurants are still a good buy. Don't ignore the omnipresent hamburger and pizza chains that kids and your pocketbook love. There may be restaurants where the kids get a show by watching the cooking, such as Japanese steak houses where they make the dinner on a grill right at the table. Or pancake houses where the cook performs by tossing flapjacks into the air.

Swimming   If there's no beach or lake nearby, check municipal pools or family programs at the local "Y."

Bird watching   Arm yourself with the Roger Tory Peterson "Field Guide" for your region. The National Audubon Society or your local library can also suggest aids.

Rock collecting   Even ordinary stones which are speckled with various types of material fascinate little kids.

Shell collecting   The beaches are filled with an infinite variety of shell designs.

Insect collecting   This includes butterflies.

Picnicking   You can combine this with a day at a lake or at the beach.

Sightseeing   This is the only way a lot of New York fathers ever get to see the Statue of Liberty.

Camping   Assuming you have the basic equipment and don't have to lay out a lot of money for this overnight bash. Some camping supply stores rent equipment.

Horseback riding   Even if you don't ride, they might enjoy being taken to a stable where they can take an hour's ride.

Hiking   Even a one or two hour trek through the woods can be fun for the kids. Take along a bird or plant identification book. You can pick up inexpensive paperbacks at any bookstore.

Fishing   This can be part of a camping trip or the activity for an all-day outing.

Biking   The increased popularity of this easy sport has made bike rentals available in many towns and cities, so you don't have to own one.

Circus   This appeals to the younger ages. Older kids might be bored.

Boat rides   If you live on the water or are a short drive to the coast or a large lake or river, you will often find excursion rides. You can also rent sailboats, motor boats, rowboats, and canoes at many lakes and seashore spots.

Theatre   If you're lucky enough to live in a city where there are lots of theatres available, you'll find special children's theatres for younger kids. Many local groups in small towns often put on performances of plays kids like.

Playgrounds   Little kids are often quite happy if you take them to a playground equipped with swings, slides, and climbing rigs. Plus they usually find their peers to play with.

Zoo   The kid may already feel he's living in one, but try the authentic type on him.

Museums   Besides art museums, there are those devoted to science, natural history, Indians, crafts, and many other special interests.

Amusement parks   These are becoming rare. Some city parks maintain merry-go-rounds which still enchant youngsters.

Ice skating   On a lake or pond is nice; artificial ice rinks are fine too.

Going for a drive   There are farms where city kids can see farm animals. Fall foliage time is an excuse for buying apples right at the orchard. Some let you pick your own. The itinerary can be as simple as you like.

Playing ball   Gauge your own muscle tone before you slide into this one.

Shopping   Do this only if there is a definite purpose. Help the kids buy gifts for each other or for their mother's birthday, Christmas, or for special occasions. There are many special interest shops, like craft shops, pet shops, or hardware stores that become fascinating expeditions.

Trip to a junkyard   You'd be surprised at what you find. Just don't plan to cart it all home.

Snow skiing   Equipment can be rented. Many ski shops run day or weekend trips which include transportation, lodging, and lessons. But skiing is expensive, even if you own equipment and provide your own transportation.

Water skiing   Motor boats and water skis are available for rental at most lakes. If skis are not available for rental, it may be a good investment for the summer to buy a few pairs.

Ocean liners   If you're near a seaport, check arrival and departure schedules of ocean liners. Visitors are allowed on board prior to sailing.

TV stations   Many TV stations run conducted tours for visitors. Also inquire about shows which allow an audience during the taping or telecast.

Visiting your office   Little kids are fascinated by the place where daddy works. Typewriters, adding machines, hole punchers, staplers, and a seemingly endless supply of blank paper and pencils can keep them entertained for hours. Watch so they don't interfere with other employees or take them on Saturday.

Kite flying   You can make your own or buy one. Kites come in many fantastic shapes and colors.

Local papers often list weekend activities for children. Consult them for ideas. Be sure they are well described so that you know what you are getting into.

Occasionally ask the kids to bring one of their friends along. This is a good idea when you have only one child. The kids are then quite happy playing with one another and you get a respite. Don't do it regularly. It interferes with the growth of your own relationship.

If you have more than one child, try to give each of them a little time alone with you on each visit. One may have something to talk over with you that he or she is reticent about in front of others.

Also, occasionally have only one child at a time visit so that each gets the chance to have you all alone.

Beware of turning your visits into a command appearance on the part of the children. Though you are entitled to regular vists, the kids may have something extra special to do at the same time that would preclude seeing you. Excuse them that weekend and try to grab a couple of hours during the week. Besides, deep down you might like having the weekend all to yourself—and what's wrong with that?

9

Me Tarzan.
You Jane.
This My Apartment.

So here you are a bachelor in your own pad. Just like in the movies. It's like you're Cary Grant. Especially if you pull in your stomach a little.

Now a great deal of your ease with entertaining women in your apartment depends on your background. By that I mean your extramarital sex life. If you did a lot of one-to-one entertaining while you were married, this chapter will tell you little that's new. All you're doing now is providing your own motel room.

That's exactly what happened to Joe. Here he was in his late thirties, good looking, vigorous and divorced. Like many married men he found that one of the first casualties of his disintegrating marriage was sex. So he sought it elsewhere and readily found it. After divorce, he merely continued his pleasures without fear of adultery. Having his own apartment just made it less complicated.

135

If your extramarital adventures were limited, if not damned infrequent, you can develop from there. And then, of course, there are those few men who remained faithful to those few wives who remained faithful to them. If you're one of those, you have everything to learn.

Let me first explain that as a single man you get a lot more attention than you might expect. It isn't that you necessarily look better, though you may if you've just been released from an unhappy marriage. It's that, as I pointed out earlier, you are a favorable statistic. There are less of you (single man) than there are of her (single woman). The older you are, the more favorable your market situation.

As a single man you are not expected to entertain. You could go through your whole single life cleaning and cooking only for yourself and, if you have any, your visiting children.

But look around you. A lot of single men entertain in their apartments.

It may be as simple as asking someone from the office to stop off for a drink after work, asking the guys to play poker at your apartment, or as involved as asking a date and another couple up for dinner. It's the area in between where you hit paydirt: having a date up for dinner.

There's one great advantage to having a woman up to your apartment for dinner. It's "something to do." Let me explain. An unexpected problem of dating when you become single again is the business of always having to be "on." You always have to keep the conversation going, be entertaining, sparkling. If you're not hyperthyroid, this can wear you down. After doing this with date after date, you long to just relax, shut up and read a newspaper for a few minutes. She doubtless longs for the same thing.

Of course, once you get to know each other better, having to be "on" passes. But in the beginning you must fill the time with witty talk, handstands, or something. The "something" could be an activity that shuts you both up while you go through those initial times of just getting used to one another. It could be a movie or theatre. Or it could be making dinner at home. You're busy with dinner. She may or may not help you. (I'll discuss that later.) But it gets you over the hurdle of having to be "on."

As I mentioned before, many men resort to entertaining women in their homes for another major reason: lack of money. It's cheaper to feed two at home than it is to continually foot restaurant bills for two.

One aspect of single living that confronts men is loneliness. You get up in the morning alone. Okay, so far. Maybe you're one of those people who doesn't feel very communicative first thing in the morning. You spend the day at work. Then dinner, often alone. At least preparing and eating dinner provides a distraction. But once you finish with the dishes, you face an evening alone. You could go to a movie . . . alone. Watch TV . . . alone. There are a lot of activities you can do alone. But alone is alone and too much is too much. It's nice to be with somebody.

So you make a date. That usually means dinner. Maybe you first meet at a bar for a drink beforehand. Throw in a movie or theatre. With your wife, you could call that an evening and head home. But with a date, it's sometimes awkward to head straight home from the movie or theatre. So you stop in a bar for a drink. Or maybe you postponed dessert from dinner until after the show. No matter how you plan it, it adds up to a pretty expensive evening.

Now what's your choice? Do you go out or do you stay home . . . alone? You've got another option. You ask the lady up for dinner.

A lot of guys would turn this down as revealing themselves to the ladies as a cheapskate. Wrong! What most men don't realize is that a woman living alone goes through similar agonies. Too much alone is too much. It's a helluva lot nicer to be with someone. And it doesn't have to be a big night on the town. She knows that if you're divorced or separated you may be maintaining two homes and therefore may not have a lot of spare cash for entertaining. If you're a young single college or working man she probably realizes your financial status may be on a par with hers. She's perfectly happy to just go to a movie, take a walk, or have dinner at your apartment.

It's true that there are some women who only want to be "taken out." In a society where men can still move about more freely than women, you become her instrument of access to places she would prefer not to go alone or with other women. This cultural role-playing is fortunately disappearing, especially among younger people. But among those over 35 it still persists. It's as much the fault of the men as it is of the women. If your attitude is that you're "buying" the lady's time by giving her a gift of an evening out, she'll end up with more interest in what you do for her than in what you are. But if you make it clear that you are with her because of your interest in her as a person, she won't care if all you do is spend the evening sharing a candy bar.

One Spring weekend Roger happened to be a little short of funds and decided to pull in his horns on entertainment costs. So he phoned Marsha for a date and suggested they simply take a walk, have dinner at a Chinese restaurant (even the best are usually not too expensive), and take in a movie. Marsha's reply was, "A movie? That's not much." Roger brought the conversation to an abrupt halt. He hasn't called Marsha since. She probably set out immediately in search of a new free ride.

Of course, this whole problem arises because, except among younger people, it is assumed that the man pays for the evening's expenses. There are few women, even among those who claim to be "liberated," who have gotten around to liberating their pocketbooks. It's the rare woman who would be willing to share the costs of an evening with a man, even when they have comparable incomes. This lopsided arrangement curtails many men's social life. It's too expensive to go out often. So entertaining at your own apartment is an alternative.

A woman going to a man's apartment is no longer someone people snicker at. Maybe some of your old-fashioned married friends still do. It's one way they reassure themselves they are stuck in the best of all possible worlds. The single world you now belong to is vastly different. Single people, even older single people, are much more casual about social arrangements than married folks.

They move about more easily. They are much freer in their relationships.

This freedom includes not only casual entertaining. It includes sexual relationships. I'll explain.

First, let's talk about entertaining the lady in your apartment. There are a few ground rules you'll have to observe.

The first is to recognize the fact that if you're uncomfortable or embarrassed, you're not the first man to feel this way. After all, think of where you are in your life. If you were married, you spent all those years living with one woman in a home. Now you have your own home and you're asking a woman to visit. Perhaps you genuinely like her and are not solely interested in scoring. You want to make a good impression. It's almost impossible for you not to be self-conscious in these circumstances.

The woman may also be self-conscious about her visit. After all, she doesn't know what you expect of her. Are you setting up a seduction for which she may not be ready? If she likes you, she wants the evening to go well too.

Mike had two dates with Cynthia. Once they had gone dancing after dinner. The other time they had gone to the theatre. He wanted to see her again but his daughter's dental bills precluded a big night on the town. He suggested dinner at his apartment. Cynthia readily accepted.

Mike was as nervous as an understudy checking the star's temperature. He bought fresh flowers for the living room. He had noticed that on previous dates Cynthia had usually ordered a particular Italian aperitif. He bought a bottle. When Cynthia arrived, he offered her a drink. His forethought about the apertif didn't escape her notice. She thanked him for his thoughtfulness and gently kissed him on the cheek. Mike's stage fright disappeared. Dinner and the evening were a huge success.

Let's assume you're going all out. You're going to make dinner for two. How much should you involve the lady with helping you make dinner? If she's someone you've been seeing regularly and she's been to your apartment before, there's no problem. You'll probably make dinner together. We're discussing world premieres: the first time you invite her for dinner.

Let me tell you what happened to a friend of mine. Don made a date to meet a lady Saturday afternoon. They were going to visit a museum, window-shop, take in an early movie, and then return to his apartment for dinner. Well, Don found he had free time in the morning. So he set the table, cleaned the vegetables, prepared the salad . . . in short, he did everything he could conceivably think of. His bright idea was that when they returned to his apartment together there would be nothing to do. They could relax over a couple of drinks while the steak was broiling. Good idea? The lady didn't think so. She was either caught up in traditional role-playing in which the kitchen is woman's domain, not the man's, or she felt cut out from participation by Don's elaborate arrangements. If her reaction was the latter, she may have considered herself relegated to being Don's dinner guest instead of his dinner companion. The lady sulked, dutifully ate her dinner, complained of fatigue, and asked to be taken home early.

Don had neglected to make dinner a cooperative project. He never let the woman get involved. Naturally, she never let him get involved either.

Newton, on the other hand, turned an honest problem he had into an opportunity to invite Ann up to his apartment for dinner on a basis she could graciously accept.

Newton found he enjoyed cooking but he faced wide gulfs of ignorance. Cookbook instructions were often too subjective for him. Such cautions as "when the butter is good and hot" left him at sea because he didn't know when the butter in his skillet was duplicating the image the author had in mind. He ran aground a couple of times trying to make veal scallopine. Veal scallops being tricky to sauté, his always came out curled, well done, and tough.

He suggested to Ann that he buy enough veal scallops for the two of them and that she demonstrate to him in his kitchen the proper method for sautéing them. It was simple psychology. He made Ann feel needed, so she agreed to help him make dinner at his apartment.

Newton's original excuse formed the basis for a series of evenings in which they made dinner together. Often, they would spend Saturday afternoon together and shop for dinner on the way back to Newton's apartment.

If a problem arises, it isn't always the man's fault. Ross spent a day with a woman who made it quite clear that she was "liberated" after being married for years to a man who treated her as an executive maid. When they ended up at Ross's apartment for dinner, she was apparently still getting even with her husband. All Ross's suggestions that she help by setting the table or some similar chore were playfully pushed aside. So Ross did all the work while the lady enjoyed the luxury of having a butler. He hasn't called her again because he doesn't feel like catering dinner for her. Of course, many men never volunteer to help women who have invited them to dinner. They just sit back expecting to be waited on.

So, as a general rule, when you invite the lady up for dinner, give her the option of helping you. If you want to show off your cooking expertise, she won't mind. Ask her to set the table or make the salad. Let her do something—if she wants to. Your attitude should be of sharing experiences; of helping one another. It's more fun when you do things together.

Naturally, there are exceptions. If your dinner companion is a mother with small children for whom she must cook three meals a day, seven days a week, she'll probably be delighted to perch on your kitchen stool nursing a drink while you put dinner together. She's on vacation. But even here you might ask her to put on some records or mix a fresh batch of drinks for the two of you. Let her be more than just a spectator.

You may run into one special problem if you were married and have remained in the house where you and your wife lived together. The lady may be reluctant or a bit uneasy about working in another woman's kitchen.

Don't worry too much about how good the dinner is unless you're really into cooking. Remember, you're just having dinner with a friend, not an inspector from Guide Michelin.

Dinner is only part of the evening's entertainment. What do you do for the rest of the time? This is not a silly question. Many men are nervous, filled with anxieties when they first start inviting women up to their apartments.

A lot of men resuming social relations with women after a divorce run aground on unexpected difficulties. No matter how talented you were in bed when you were married, if your wife called it quits on the marriage, you could face a problem that never occurred to a jock like you: impotence. It happens often. Thankfully, it passes once you regain new confidence in yourself. If it persists, seek professional help. If the marriage languished in its final months or years with sexual abstinence, you may have lost confidence in yourself as a lover.

But even if you have no problems, you may still be nervous. First, just because the lady accepted an invitation to your apartment doesn't imply she's going to be your bed partner. That doesn't mean she won't be—just don't take it for granted.

The whole idea of being nervous may sound silly to some men, but to many it's a real factor. American mythology has created the image of all men as suffering from acute satyriasis. T'aint so. Much connubial bliss is lost not just because the wife is burdened with Victorian notions of sex being dirty; a lot of men never progressed beyond fumbling in the back seat of a car. It takes two to make a mistake in bed.

But assume your virility is intact. Those of us who went into marriage before the so-called sexual freedom of today's young people went laden with a lot of inhibitory baggage. Your sex life progressed at some sort of pace. In longlasting marriages, there are few couples who can claim that their sex life is still lusty, joyous, little more than dutiful, or, possibly, even in existence. A lot of magic goes out of marriages after awhile. In fact, more people than realize it talk themselves into the fact that the magic is there to begin with.

An additional problem men face is that they feel they are expected to perform. They assume seduction is part of the scenario. After all, you're not a man unless you at least try. It's a role publicized by popular culture that many men feel they must live up to. To listen to many men talk among themselves, you wonder that their zippers haven't developed a conditioned reflex to open every time a woman walks by.

As a single, particularly if you're in the initial period after your marriage has dissolved, you don't have to cast yourself as a stud. You may well be burdened with the honest self-appraisal that your marriage bed wouldn't exactly have earned you a Ph.D. from Masters and Johnson. Not that you couldn't be doctorate material. So relax with the lady. It's perfectly possible you may want to just enjoy her company at the beginning. Let the relationship progress naturally.

Tony had several dates with Betty. Both had come out of previous marriages with scarred egos. Both felt unsure of themselves as bed partners and neither had had a sexual experience since their marriages. They enjoyed each other's company, were attracted to each other, and each knew privately that they would become lovers once they overcame the hurdles of fear and timidity.

Tony's apartment was the obvious place. One evening Betty came up for dinner. That they would go to bed that evening was unsaid but understood by both of them. And they were both nervous about how to start the trek to the bedroom without fear or tension.

They lingered over an after-dinner drink. Tony put on some records, including a couple of favorites of both of them. They danced, necked while dancing. Then Tony, just knowing the moment was there, turned off the record player. The evening was a success for both of them.

Arthur, on the other hand, entertained women frequently in

his apartment. But he endured several shattering failures in his bedroom before he was able to return to a healthy sex life.

Now, before I scare you into thinking you're doomed to a life of celibacy unless you're careful, let's talk about the pleasures— because they are there. And in a manner that will delight and surprise you.

The nice thing about being single again as an adult is that in the pursuit of women you are far beyond the pawing and groping of adolescence.

Regardless of how fumbling a lover you were as a husband, you bring with you experience and some sophistication. And, of course, if your sex life with your wife was good, you're way ahead.

Not only do you enter into single relationships with a fresh adult attitude. The lady does too. You're not the only one who realizes you're both grown-up, full of healthy desires that you would like to satisfy. The lady knows it about herself too. And she's a lot less inhibited than she was when she was younger and sex was a strange new world. She's certainly a lot less inhibited than many married women for whom sex has become a joyless routine.

Perhaps it's the permissive age in which we live. Perhaps, for formerly married women, it's release from an unhappy marriage. Whatever the cause, you'll find that lovemaking can be freer, less inhibited and vastly more delightful than you had anticipated. You're two people who like each other and say to each other, ''Let's have fun.''

Incidentally, if you figure she may stay over, have the fore-thought to stock up with the necessities for breakfast for two.

10

Pets, Pains and People

There are a few other areas of living alone that you must now handle.

One is pets. Should you own one? If you are hooked on dogs or cats, there is little that can be done to dissuade you from committing yourself to owning one. But committed you are!

When you live alone a pet fills the need for having another breathing object other than yourself around the house. However, a pet is also a greater responsibility when you are its sole companion, playmate, food source, walker (for dogs), and toilet trainer. You cannot casually decide not to go home from work when you have an animal that needs some tending.

Older animals require less care, but kittens and puppies are initially a burden. Are you willing to accept it? It's possible to arrange for other people to do this for you, but be prepared to pay. If you have a cleaning person, she can take over on the days she's in. You might find a teenager or a senior citizen in your

145

apartment house or neighborhood who would be happy to make a little extra money by taking care of your pet while you're out. In some cities there are dog walking services that will pick up your dog on a regularly maintained schedule, give him a good walk and return the dog to your apartment.

If you decide to go away for a weekend or on a vacation, you've got to make plans for boarding your pet. Some people are able to leave cats alone overnight. Dogs are obviously a different problem. Once your dog is trained, not only toilet trained but trained to have good manners with people, friends might volunteer to dog-sit. If not, there are kennels. It's a good idea to check out the kennel before you use it. Too many people have had the sad experience of getting their pets back dirty or sick. For dogs, be sure the kennel has runs so that the animal gets some exercise.

Once you get your pet down to a feeding schedule of once-a-day, feed him in the morning. You're always home in the morning. Some people must like to build a little anxiety into their lives by creating the problem of having to get home in the evening to feed their pets. Morning feeding avoids this.

When you're single, a pet spends a lot of time alone. This is no reason to feel guilty. They just sleep a lot. But you should compensate by playing with them when you are home and, in the case of dogs, giving them long walks to assure proper exercise. It's especially important that you train your dog to live with people and not vice versa. Because the dog is alone so much, you may want to take him along with you when you visit. Most people won't object as long as your dog's visit doesn't end up with a redecorating problem. Remember, you love your pet; most other people tolerate him.

If you're a male chauvinist who likes the idea of a woman lying at your feet, then a dog may prove an ample surrogate. If you want a relationship that progresses beyond that, pets have definite limitations. With pets, you do all the talking in return for which they either look at you quizzically, lick, or utter whatever their sound is. Hopefully, you find this wanting. So you have to go out and meet people.

Dog walking is one method. Dog owners have a ritual that is very personal about their dogs, very impersonal about themselves. They exchange dogs' names, ages, breeds, feeding habits and names of veterinarians. But they offer little, if any, information about themselves. A little enterprise can push beyond animal familiarity so you can find out about the owner. If your dogs refuse to cooperate by snarling at one another, you've hit a bit of an impasse. Move on to the next dog with an appealing woman at the other end of the leash.

If you are a single man simply setting up your own pad, you probably already have a social life. Continue as before. But if you were married, former friends are not always the answer. Some of them may have "chosen sides," preferring your wife to you. So much for them. Except for your very closest married friends, you will find yourself seeing people from your former life less and less. They're just into a different scene than you are now.

So how do you meet new people? The first, and most obvious, is where you work. Are there people among your peers who are also single? The single women now take on a new interest for you. If there are other single men, find out how they spend their time away from the office. You might start a new friendship.

In larger cities there are "singles" bars. For younger people these are fun. For older people, they often turn out to be a dreary experience: a lot of 35-year-old college seniors who still think they can turn the head of the prom queen. But some bars are low-key, friendly. It may be a place in your neighborhood where local people gather. It may be a piano bar where the patrons come because they enjoy the music and meeting someone is a serendipity.

Adult education programs in public schools and colleges bring together people of similar interests. The range of courses is almost endless. Besides the standard academic subjects in the arts and sciences, adult education programs offer a wide variety of studies appealing to special interests.

You can find courses in investing, urban planning, speed reading, ecology. There are workshops in photography, film, television, dance, graphic arts and theater. Foreign lanuages range from French to Swahili.

Just as you are learning to cope with housekeeping as a single man, many women are learning to handle areas formerly considered male domains. You'll find many women enrolling for courses in auto maintenance and repair. Men are considered instinctively knowledgeable about cars. However, few possess hard-core knowledge beyond dexterity in turning on the ignition. But, if the lady doesn't know that, just keep a lesson ahead of her and you're an expert.

Contact your local public school system or colleges. In some localities, business and professional organizations often offer courses to cover materials of specific interest to their particular groups.

Yoga, karate, or judo give you a chance to get your own body in shape while meeting women trying to solve the same problem. Many "Y's" run exercise classes for adults.

You don't have to be an actor to join a local theater group. They also need people to build and paint scenery, handle lighting, work on publicity and run down to the corner for coffee. Political clubs bring together people with a reasonably common point of view on what's wrong with the way things are being run. If you find someone with whom you agree on politics, you'll be hard pressed to find an area where you seriously disagree.

There are also organizations for formerly married people. One of the best known is Parents Without Partners. They are nationwide. Their programs include social activities as well as discussion groups in which people deal with common problems. Some activities include children; some do not. In New York there is a men's club called SWorD (Single, Widowed, or Divorced). The members call themselves Swordsmen, a sobriquet that smacks of male chauvinism.

It should be apparent that there are endless choices besides peepshows.

If there are people from your former life you want to continue seeing, it's your responsibility to maintain these relationships. In the past your wife probably functioned as social secretary. Now you do it. If you exchanged Christmas or birthday gifts with certain friends or relatives, continue the practice. Keep in touch, if that's what you want.

Your reasons can be purely selfish. If you're ill and confined to bed, it's good to be able to call on a friend to shop for some food, pick up your laundry, or even bring over a ready-cooked dinner.

You should keep a telephone book with emergency numbers in case you are alone, need help, and can't reach anyone you know. Many cities maintain emergency phone numbers for police, doctors, dentists, poison control, pharmacists, and even veterinarians.

Of course, your medicine cabinet should be stocked with essentials. Keep the following on hand:

aspirin	mild laxative
antiseptic	talcum powder
boric acid	cotton-tipped swabs
sodium bicarbonate	camphor stick
adhesive tape	absorbent cotton (in sheets or
gauze	balls)
antacid	emery board
thermometer	cuticle scissor
rubbing alcohol	band-aids in a variety of sizes
vaseline	eye cup
toothpaste (keep an extra tube	tampons (the lady will be
on hand)	stunned by your forethought)
toothbrush (have a new one on	cold cream (so she can remove
hand for unexpected over-	makeup)
night guests)	

That takes care of minor bodily damage.

11
Have I Got a Girl for You!

I've mentioned earlier that as a single man in our society you enjoy the status of being a favorable statistic. That doesn't mean you should start putting benches out in your hall in anticipation of the lineup. But it does give you advantages.

Unless you are a known carrier of bubonic plague or the town eunuch, you will be sought after. It's not a bad feeling. Even though you know the statistical reason why, your ego fattens up a little.

So here you are being wanted for the first time by someone other than the Internal Revenue Service. Couple that with having your own pad in which you are evolving a life-style all your own. It's a nice setup.

Living alone is sometimes lonely. Particularly if you're used to having someone around, even with stovepipe curlers in her hair. But it isn't all bad. You have an independence which you will learn to relish. After all these years, you are suddenly on your own.

You can decide to go to a movie, take a walk, sit around, with just a towel wrapped around your middle, sipping a martini. When you get home from work, you decide how long to make your cocktail hour. *Then* you start dinner. So what if you don't finish the dishes until 10 o'clock. Is it anybody else's business? And I know a lot of people will chirp up with, "But look at your wife. She's got the kids to feed, put to bed, etcetera, etcetera." It's true and her circumstances are not to be belittled. We're just discussing the fact that you are fortunate in that most of the nights you are a free agent and can do what you please.

Surprising as it may seem, some of your married friends are going to change their attitudes toward you. The fact that you will change your attitude toward them is a separate subject.

They will probably start off by feeling sorry for poor old you. And the longer you maintain your hotel room/corner-hamburger-joint status, the longer you sustain their sympathy. But once you set up your own pad, start entertaining friends, and begin to feel and act years younger, watch out. A lot of your married friends aren't going to like it. How can it be so good for you when they are still wallowing in their compromises?

You see, with time you will find yourself feeling different about many of your married friends. After all, over the years a lot of marriages and their social scenes become habit. And you've kicked the habit. A lot of those married get-togethers are a bore. It's a way to kill the evening, an endless Round Robin of whose turn it is to have everyone over.

Not only men feel this way. One upper middle class woman who has been divorced about a year confessed that she finds herself relating less and less to her married friends. She discovered that when she went to dinner parties given by her married friends the women were dressing as status symbols for their husbands, wearing their Puccis, their Guccis, their Kenneth Lane hardware hanging from their ears, arms, and necks. She used to do the same thing, but now she just dresses to please herself and look good, something she does admirably well.

Once you've established yourself as a single man, word gets around fast. The women figure you're ripe for the plucking. And if you have your own pad, fixed up the way you like it, complete with kitchen privileges, sure you're ripe for plucking. But *you* call the harvest time.

Hardly a week will pass that someone won't suggest some lady they think you might like. At the beginning, the recommendations will be particularly frequent. Most of them will come from married women friends. They're aware of the problems single women face. Married men are involved in a fantasy world of, "Boy, if I were single, the chicks I would line up!" And they figure since you are single, you must be living what they only dream. Of course, you know it ain't so. Many evenings are spent washing your socks.

Now, it's true some guys make out immediately. They are stars in bed. And after all, they figure, isn't that all that counts? The fact that they don't relate to the woman any more than a Labrador dog to a bitch in heat is besides the point . . . to them. But a lot of men want to be more than just good bed partners. They regret that their marriages went awry and want a woman they can enjoy being with when they are both in a vertical position.

About these women whose names are going to be offered to you. You might as well make some decisions about what you think you would like and ask some questions. Are you 50 and are they offering someone of 24? Do you like bright women? Do bleached blondes turn you off? Is it important that she be pretty? You might as well do a little preliminary screening and save yourself and her a boring evening.

Your own instincts should help you decide how to judge the women suggested to you on the basis of who's doing the suggesting. But sometimes you should gamble if you want to gambol.

Marvin, a divorced friend of mine, had repeatedly parried any suggestions from his friends, Ruth and Peter, that he call Alice. Alice was billed as "attractive, bright, and a lot of fun." Marvin was reluctant because his attitude toward Ruth and Peter was changing. Sure they were nice people, but he found himself no longer interested in their "married talk." He felt freer, less settled, more open to new ideas than they. And why not? He was embarking on a new life. What he didn't need was some friend of Ruth and Peter's who would probably like to sit around talking about the kids, the house, school, or other conversational props.

One weekend Marvin found himself with nothing to do. No one to call. So he figured, to hell with it. Why not? He'd call Alice. Surprise! Alice had the same misgivings about him. She too had begun to think more as a "single" than as a formerly married lady with two kids and a house in the suburbs. Once they stashed away their mutual preconceptions, Marvin and Alice hit it off fine and have often dated since.

Friends are just one source of meeting women. The Family will have a lot of input to offer. If you travel alone you will be an object of great curiosity. Naturally, any women traveling alone who are in the same place as you will be interested in you. And they will have a natural ally in married women present. Many married women can't resist maintaining their amateur status as matchmakers. A single man is a mutant, a heretic, a backslider, a waste, a shame.

If someone is insistent you take the phone number of Amy Available, do so. It's easier than explaining why you don't want to. You can mislay it, throw it away, or swallow it. If they ask later whether you called, tell them you spent a weekend together in a Turkish bath and she sweats too much.

In the beginning you may be shy, or at least uncomfortable, about dating. There's one simple way to get through this difficult period. If friends suggest you call a woman whom they are sure you would like and if you are open to the suggestion, arrange for the four of you to go out to dinner together. You could even suggest that the evening start with drinks at your apartment.

Nobody expects you to wow them with an array of hors d'oeuvres to accompany the drinks. Peanuts, potato chips, salami chunks with mustard, store-bought paté or cheese with some crackers . . . the list of open-it-up-and-dump-it-on-a-dish edibles is endless. Modern civilization has reduced many activities to effortlessness on our part.

The presence of the other couple acts as a cushion to ease the evening. If the lady appeals to you, you can then call her on your own. If not, so it's an evening.

Favorable statistic or not, now that you're single you might take a look at yourself. Few women are so hungry for male companionship that they'll go out with any man. You may be closer to being "any man" than you realize. As long as you're on the hunt, it's difficult to creep up on your prey if it takes a giant sequoia tree to hide your girth.

An unhappy marriage gave you no incentive to try to improve your appearance. The time is now. Nobody loves a fat man except a cannibal. Even if you aren't fat but have just let a few unnecessary pounds attach themselves like barnacles, now's the time to shed them.

Just because you're past 35, paunchy and wearing glasses doesn't mean that's the way it's got to be. Medical science isn't extending our life span to give you a few more years to carry that extra weight around. The glasses have to stay (although with a less middle-aged style of frames you may *see* the same and *look* a lot better). If you insist on maximum standards for the women you would like to date, what makes you think women don't expect the same?

Leonard had left a long, unhappy marriage. He moved out with all his clothes and once in his new apartment he took a look at himself in the (wide) mirror and admitted, "My God, I've got enough for two of me!" He immediately started to diet, with sensible advice from his doctor. He joined the YMCA where he entered an exercise class. He swam in the pool. He jogged around the track. He even bought a bicycle on which he whisked around town.

After a year Leonard looked terrific. He lost 37 pounds. He was happy. His tailor, who planned an early retirement on the cost of altering Leonard's clothes, was happy too. Leonard not only looks different. He acts different. He's a single man on the town. Some of his flabby married male friends think he's acting too young for his age. No. All he did was make himself look a lot younger for his age.

So here you are slimmed down, living in your own apartment, hopefully cooking your own meals, taking care of yourself. You could keep this up forever. And you may want to.

You'll get a lot of flack from friends and family who will warn you you're not getting any younger—a man needs a woman—it's not good to live alone. It's not true. Sure, some people need the constant presence and devotion of someone else. You may not be one of those people. All you may want is to be able to spend time with someone now and then. If your married friends don't believe that, ask them how much time they'd like to spend *away* from each other.

Now that you're living alone you can start a whole new social life. You can select new friends that only you like. You can meet lots of new women, many of whom you will enjoy and will enjoy you. Invite them up to the apartment. You're the only one you have to consult. If even your best friends introduce you to some woman, you don't have to pick up the cue. It's their problem, not yours.

You're freer than you've been in years. Free to set a life-style that's strictly yours. And for you ex-married men, you've got what most people never get—a second chance.